ANCIENT CIVILIZATIONS

CHINA • INDIA • AFRICA • MESOPOTAMIA

Wendy Conklin

NEW YORK • TORONTO • LONDON • AUCKLAND • SYDNEY **Teaching**
MEXICO CITY • NEW DELHI • HONG KONG • BUENOS AIRES *Resources*

DEDICATION

To my husband, Blane, whose expertise in ancient Near Eastern languages continues to inspire me.

Acknowledgements

The author would like to thank the Oriental Institute at the University of Chicago for access to their Mesopotamian gallery.

Edited by Wendy Vierow

Cover design by Jason Robinson
Cover photo by Werner Forman/Art Resource, NY
Interior design by Sydney Wright
Interior illustration by Reneé Daily
Interior photos by David Nemelka (pages 12, 24, and 25) and Wendy Conklin (page 92)

ISBN 0-439-53993-5

CONTENTS

Africa

Mesopotamia

AN INTRODUCTION TO ANCIENT CIVILIZATIONS:
China, India, Africa, Mesopotamia

Thousands of years ago, four civilizations began and flourished in different parts of the world—China, India, Africa, and Mesopotamia. This book covers these ancient civilizations, all of which developed along rivers.

CHINA China has the oldest continuous civilization, with a written history dating back thousands of years. China's dynasties began with the Shang dynasty around 1766 BC. Among the many ancient sights in China are the Great Wall and the Grand Canal. The first major construction on the Great Wall began during the Qin dynasty under Shi Huangdi, China's first emperor, whose rule began in 221 BC. This emperor also constructed a clay army consisting of more than 7,500 men, horses, and chariots that were buried with him in a vast underground grave. The ancient Chinese were ingenious inventors, who created such items as paper, seismographs, silk, wheelbarrows, and compasses. They also used pictograph writing, which eventually developed into the characters used today. For recreation, they played games such as Go, which involves skilled strategy. Legends, such as that of the woman warrior Mulan, have been handed down throughout time. The Chinese lived life by practicing philosophical systems such as Confucianism and Taoism.

INDIA The Indus Valley Civilization, also known as ancient India, began to flourish around 2500 BC. It was located in parts of what are now India and Pakistan. Because the writing system of the Indus Valley people has not been deciphered, many mysteries of this civilization are yet to be revealed. Archaeologists remain hopeful that a bilingual tablet will be found so that the ancient Indus Valley pictographs can be translated. Although the writing system has not been decoded, the architecture and artifacts of ancient India reveal much about its people. The Indus Valley people built organized cities with buildings—some of which included sewage and plumbing systems. They used small, decorated seals for trading and identification purposes. By 1700 BC, the Indus Valley civilization began to decline—perhaps due to both natural causes and war. Around 1500 BC, Aryans from central Asia invaded India and influenced India's culture. India's Vedic period lasted from about 1500 BC to 200 BC. During this time, the Aryans created four major categories of castes. Great literature was written down, including the great epics of the *Mahabharata* and the *Ramayana*.

These epic poems tell of stories involving Hindu gods. Although most Indians practiced Hinduism, some practiced Buddhism, which was founded around 500 BC by a teacher called Siddhartha Gautama, later known as Buddha. A few hundred years later, India had its first great emperor, Chandragupta Maurya, who founded the Maurya empire.

 AFRICA Most people know about the ancient civilization of Egypt, but few know about its sometime rival, Kush, which flourished around 2000 BC. Kush, a part of ancient Nubia, was located in what is now northern Sudan. Like Egypt, this civilization included homes and cities along the world's longest river, the Nile. Kush was an important trading center and exported goods including gold and emeralds. The people of Kush also became expert ironworkers. They used Meroitic writing, which included an alphabet of 23 signs that could be written in hieroglyphics or cursive. For recreation, Kushites may have played Wari, an African game of strategy for two players. The histories of Egypt and Kush were intertwined for many years, with both cultures conquering each other at various times and adopting each other's customs. Each culture influenced the other's religion, and they shared many gods. Because Kushite kings were thought to be sons of the god Amun, Kushite queens were honored as mothers of gods and wives of Amun. These queens had the power to rule by themselves or equally with their husbands and sons. Kushite queens could be fierce leaders. In 24 BC, after the Roman conquerors imposed a tax on Kushites, a Kushite queen sent her army to attack. The Romans answered with an attack on the Kushites, but then signed a peace treaty with Kush. By about 400 AD, Kush had broken up into small states.

MESOPOTAMIA The Mesopotamians occupied the land between the Tigris and Euphrates rivers in what are now parts of Iraq, Syria, and Turkey. The first known inhabitants of this area date back to about 7000 BC. By about 3500 BC, the world's first known civilization had evolved. Among its many innovations were the first known map of the world and the first known system of writing—called *cuneiform*. One cuneiform tablet, dating to about 200 BC, includes the world's oldest game rules— instructions for playing the Royal Game of Ur. In addition to writing, Mesopotamians used a base 60 mathematical system with place values that included the concept of zero. Mesopotamians decorated their architecture with cone mosaics, a mosaic that consisted of small clay cones arranged in patterns. They built temples, called ziggurats, for Mesopotamian deities. These temples contained votives, or statues of worshippers with hands clasped in prayer. One of the world's most famous ziggurats was the legendary Hanging Gardens of Babylon—built by King Nebuchadnezzar II of Babylon and called one of the Seven Wonders of the Ancient World. There were many gods and goddesses for whom these ziggurats were built. Mesopotamians believed that their deities controlled different aspects of nature. The deities also played a part in Mesopotamian literature. One of the world's oldest epics is the story of Gilgamesh, a king who crosses paths with the gods in his search for immortality. One Mesopotamian king, Hammurabi, expanded the kingdom and laid down Hammurabi's Code, one of the earliest sets of laws ever recorded.

HOW TO USE THIS BOOK

This book was written to give teachers a variety of activities to help students learn about the ancient civilizations of China, India, Africa, and Mesopotamia. Many of the hands-on activities encourage students to imagine what it would be like to live in the past. This resource presents information about the geography, architecture, arts, sciences, governments, and religions of these ancient civilizations in an interesting format to make learning exciting and productive. The book is divided into four sections, one for each civilization. Each section begins with a map and time line, which you may choose to reproduce for students. You may also choose to create transparencies to show to students on an overhead projector. Each section also includes background information throughout. This background information is for your use, although some activities require that you share the background information with students. It is best to work through the activities within each section consecutively, because many of the topics build upon information introduced earlier in the unit. As you introduce each civilization to students, begin by using the map and references that accompany each new section. This will help students to understand the time frame and location of each civilization.

A WARNING ABOUT WEB SITES

To accompany Internet-savvy classrooms, various Web sites that can be used to find additional information are sprinkled throughout the book. Before allowing students to investigate these Web sites, be sure to check out each one yourself to determine if it is appropriate for them.

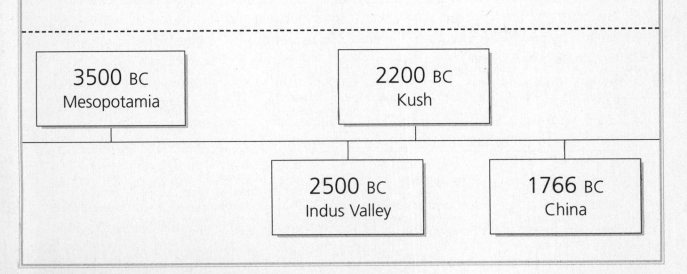

3500 BC
Mesopotamia

2200 BC
Kush

2500 BC
Indus Valley

1766 BC
China

CHINA

Map and Time Line

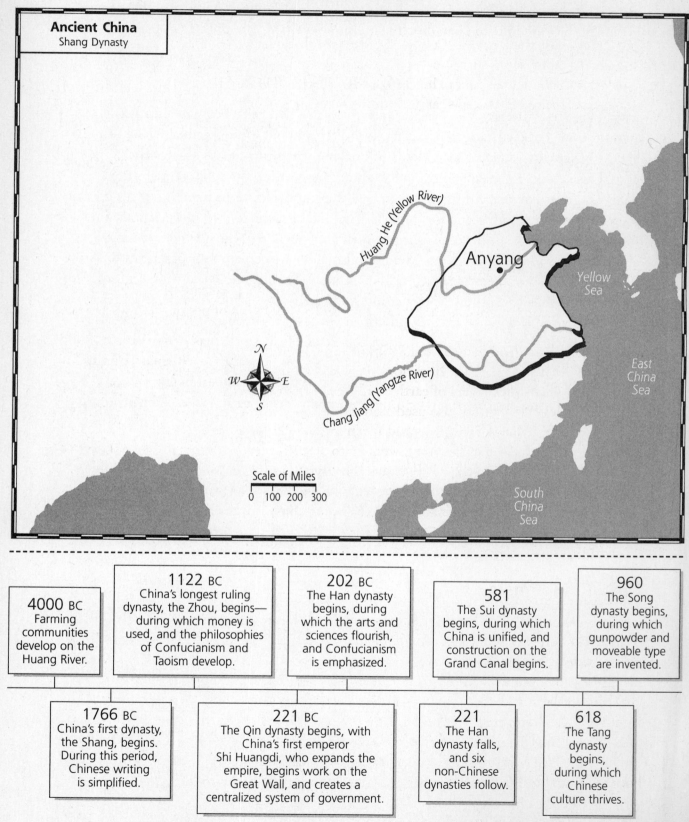

Ancient China
Shang Dynasty

Huang He (Yellow River)

Anyang

Yellow Sea

East China Sea

Chang Jiang (Yangtze River)

N
W   E
S

South China Sea

Scale of Miles
0 100 200 300

4000 BC
Farming communities develop on the Huang River.

1766 BC
China's first dynasty, the Shang, begins. During this period, Chinese writing is simplified.

1122 BC
China's longest ruling dynasty, the Zhou, begins—during which money is used, and the philosophies of Confucianism and Taoism develop.

221 BC
The Qin dynasty begins, with China's first emperor Shi Huangdi, who expands the empire, begins work on the Great Wall, and creates a centralized system of government.

202 BC
The Han dynasty begins, during which the arts and sciences flourish, and Confucianism is emphasized.

221
The Han dynasty falls, and six non-Chinese dynasties follow.

581
The Sui dynasty begins, during which China is unified, and construction on the Grand Canal begins.

618
The Tang dynasty begins, during which Chinese culture thrives.

960
The Song dynasty begins, during which gunpowder and moveable type are invented.

GEOGRAPHY AND ARCHITECTURE

Land, Water, and Landmarks

Today, China has the largest population of the world's countries and ranks third in area. China's geography varies by region and includes such features as the mountains of the Himalaya, which include Earth's highest peak—Mount Everest; two of Earth's longest rivers—the Huang He and the Yangtze; fertile farmlands of Yangtze Valley; the Gobi Desert and the Taklimakan Desert—one of Earth's driest deserts; and the beautiful limestone hills of Guilin. Tourists go to China each year to see its geographical wonders and famous historical sites, including the Forbidden City—China's largest imperial palace; Tiananmen Square—the world's largest city square; the Great Wall of China—one of the seven wonders of the world; and the terra cotta army—found in the tomb of a Qin emperor.

The Great Wall

Sometime after 214 BC, in an effort to protect the northern border of China from invaders, Emperor Shi Huangdi of the Qin dynasty began to connect and restore older walls— creating the Great Wall of China. Among the tens of thousands of people who were forced to work on the wall were soldiers, convicts, and conscripted laborers—many of whom died in the process. To build the wall, workers used a variety of materials, including stone in areas where it was plentiful. In various regions, workers compacted earth between board frames. Four-inch-thick layers of earth were placed on top of each other to create the wall. Laborers of the Han dynasty also used stones and earth to build the wall westward through the Gobi Desert. Many of the walls had fallen into disrepair, so the walls of the Qin dynasty were strengthened. Beacon towers 15 to 30 miles apart were added to the walls so that smoke signals could warn of an attack. This system relayed messages more quickly than using a rider on horseback. Bricks were not used as building materials on the Great Wall until the Ming dynasty (1368–1644). Today, at about 4,000 miles long, the Great Wall stretches from the Bo Hai Gulf of the Yellow Sea to Gansu Province in the west. It is the world's longest structure built by people.

The Grand Canal

Just as the Great Wall of China at first connected existing walls, the Grand Canal connected a series of waterways. At about 1,200 miles, it is the longest waterway in the world made by people. The canal's oldest section, known as the Southern Grand Canal, may have been built as early as 600 BC. The early canal system allowed troops to move between northern and southern China. The canals also allowed the transport of goods from the agricultural south to reach northern cities. From 607 to 610, the Sui dynasty linked the Huang Ho and Huai rivers, creating the present Grand Canal. Further work on the Grand Canal continued through subsequent dynasties. The waterway incorporates both rivers and canals and remains a transportation link in China today.

TOURING ANCIENT CHINA

Students plan a sightseeing trip through China and plot out their travel route on a map.

MATERIALS

Plotting a Map Route (page 11); books and encyclopedias, Internet access, maps of China, pencils or pens, colored markers or crayons, paper.

HERE'S HOW

❶ Tell students that they will plan a sightseeing trip to China. Explain that before students plan their tours, they need to get to know China's major landforms and sights.

❷ Distribute copies of *Plotting a Map Route* to students. Share with students the background information about China's geography on page 9.

❸ Have students research information about China's geography and tourist sights using books, encyclopedias, the Internet, and maps of China. Make sure they research the locations listed on *Plotting a Map Route*.

❹ Instruct students to map out their trip. Have them place the labels on *Plotting a Map Route* as well as other sites that they plan to visit on their maps. Then have students number the places on their maps to reflect the order in which they plan to tour the sites.

❺ Encourage students to write short blurbs about the major sites on their map. Then ask them to color their maps.

❻ Display students' travel routes around the classroom.

EXTENSION

Have students search newspapers and the Internet for airline and fare options for their trips. Ask them to think about what time of year they would like to travel and to choose the most economical tickets. You may also wish to let students design their own plane tickets or boarding passes.

Answers

Sites on students' maps may vary, but should include the labels shown on the map. Students may also include short descriptions of each site, such as the following: The Forbidden City—China's largest imperial palace; The Grand Canal—the world's longest waterway made by people; The Great Wall—one of the seven wonders of the world; The Silk Road—a trade route between China and the West; The Temple of Heaven—where emperors prayed for their people; Terra Cotta Army—a life-size, clay-figure army, which guarded the tomb of a Qin emperor; and Tiananmen Square—the world's largest city square.

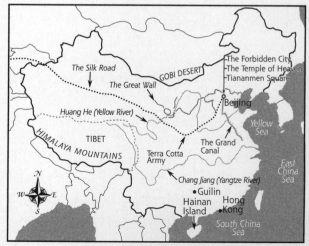

PLOTTING A MAP ROUTE

Plan a tour of ancient China. As you plan your travel route, make sure to include the famous sites listed below. Label the sites on the map. Then number your sites to reflect the order in which you plan to see them.

Beijing	Guilin	Terra Cotta Army
The Forbidden City	Hong Kong	Tiananmen Square
Gobi Desert	Huang He (Yellow River)	Yangtze River
The Grand Canal	The Silk Road	
The Great Wall	The Temple of Heaven	

Include these places on your map, but not on your tour: Hainan Island, Himalaya Mountains, Tibet, East China Sea, South China Sea, Yellow Sea.

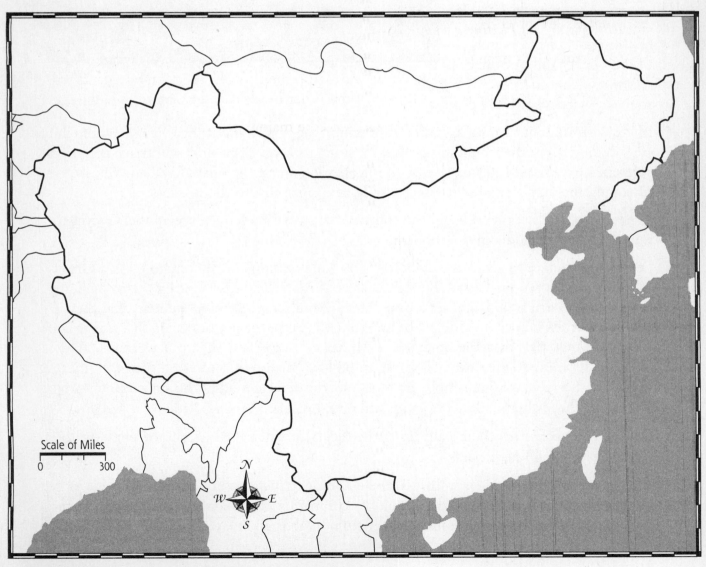

Scale of Miles
0   300

THE GREAT WALL REENACTMENT

Students create a model of a section of the Great Wall of China.

MATERIALS

recycled materials—such as cereal boxes, shoeboxes, soda cans, milk jugs, and oatmeal canisters; reference materials; Internet access; paper; pencils or pens; glue or tape

HERE'S HOW

1 The day before doing this activity, ask students to bring in recycled materials, such as cereal and shoe boxes, that could be used for building.

2 Ask students if they know anything about the origins of the Great Wall of China. Allow students to share their knowledge with the class.

© David Nemelka

3 Share with students the background information on page 9 about the Great Wall of China. Before they begin their building project let students browse through additional resources: reference books and Internet sites with information about the Great Wall and Shi Huangdi, the emperor who ordered it built, at a great cost to the workers.

4 When the class is ready to begin the construction, have students place all their recycled materials in the middle of the room.

5 Select one student to act as the emperor, who will commission workers to build a Great Wall for the classroom. Instruct the emperor to organize building groups, select building materials for each group, and set a time limit for building. (Remind students that they will work at the emperor's whim. For example, the emperor might decide that one group gets more materials than the others, or even has more workers than other groups.) The emperor should also instruct each group to build a portion of the Great Wall with the same measurements. For example, he or she might determine that the structure must be at least 12 inches high, 30 inches long, and no more than 3 inches wide.

6 Have groups construct their walls using the recycled materials. Instruct the emperor to supervise the building process.

7 After groups complete their walls, tell the emperor to inspect the walls and give his or her final approval or disapproval. Have the class compare sections and discuss the challenges each group faced. How might unequal division of labor and material distribution have affected each outcome?

THE GRAND CANAL QUIZ

Students play a quiz game about China's Grand Canal.

MATERIALS

paper, pencils, reference books including encyclopedias, Internet access, timer or clock with second hand

HERE'S HOW

1 Share with students the background information on page 9 about the Grand Canal. Then allow teams time to gather facts about the Grand Canal using encyclopedias, reference books, and the Internet.

2 When you feel students are ready to take a quiz on what they've learned, divide the class into four teams (or more if you have a large class).

3 Tell teams that you will be asking them questions about the Grand Canal. After you ask each question, allow teams fifteen seconds to agree on an answer. Then ask teams to write their answers on a piece of paper. One by one, ask teams to reveal their answers. Award teams one point for each correct answer. Repeat the process for each question. The team with the most points at the end of the game is the winner.

4 Ask teams the questions below or use questions students have written. Allow for variations in answers.

1. When did construction on the Grand Canal first begin? *(approximately 500 BC)*

2. How long is the Grand Canal? *(approximately 1,000 miles or 1,600 km)*

3. True or false: The Grand Canal is the world's largest artificial waterway. *(true)*

4. In which part of China is the Grand Canal? *(northeast)*

5. In which two directions does the Grand Canal extend? *(north and south)*

6. Why was the Grand Canal built? *(to ship grain and other goods from less populated areas in the south to more populated areas in the north)*

7. The completed Grand Canal begins and ends at which two cities? *(Hangzhou and Beijing)*

8. Under which Emperor were the largest sections of the Canal built? *(Emperor Yang Ti)*

9. What famous ruler ordered the canal to be lengthened to Beijing? *(Kublai Khan)*

10. When was construction completed on the Grand Canal? *(about 1200 AD)*

Bonus Question: Why is the Grand Canal technically not a canal? *(Canals are artificial waterways, and the Grand Canal includes parts of natural waterways.)*

Arts and Sciences

Chinese Inventions

The Chinese are responsible for many great inventions, including kites, seismographs, porcelain, and moveable type. Chinese inventions reach far back into time. Silk was created by the Chinese at least 3,000 years ago, and the first known compass, paper, and wheelbarrow were invented about 2,000 years ago. The Chinese invention of gunpowder more than 1,000 years ago was used for fireworks, signals, and weapons—which changed the system of warfare.

The Game of Go

More than 2,000 years ago, the Chinese played a game of strategy called Go. This board game, which is played by two people with black and white stones, includes a grid of nineteen horizontal and nineteen vertical lines that create 361 intersections. The object of the game is to surround and capture territory on the board, as well as to capture your opponent's stones. There are many theories about the history of the game. One suggests that Chinese leaders demanded that their soldiers practice and master this game.

Chinese Writing

Chinese writing, which dates back thousands of years, is the oldest form of writing still in use today. The earliest known Chinese writing, which consisted of pictographs, dates back about 3,500 years to the Shang dynasty. This writing appeared on oracle bones, which were mostly bones of cattle and sheep used by priests to predict the future. An official script of more-simplified characters developed during the Qin dynasty, when China's first emperor created a centralized system of writing. This script was further simplified during the third century. Later, two more styles of calligraphy developed—both of which incorporated a fluid writing style. Today, the Chinese language includes about 50,000 characters, although most people can function with a vocabulary of about 4,000 characters.

The Legend of Mulan

About 1,300 years ago, an anonymous Chinese writer wrote a poem about a heroic female warrior named Mulan. Many historians doubt Mulan's existence, but her hometown in Henan Province has monuments testifying to her life. The legend of Mulan tells that she disguised herself as a man, responded to the emperor's draft, and served in place of her ailing father and young brother. Mulan fought for twelve years in battle, and then returned home. When her comrades from the battlefield saw that she was a woman, they were shocked! After Mulan's service, the emperor wanted to appoint her to a high post. However, Mulan refused, the emperor detained her, and Mulan hung herself in an act of protest. The emperor was offended, and no accounts were written about Mulan in history books. Legends of Mulan circulated, and a novel was written about her toward the end of the Ming Dynasty (1368–1644).

CHINESE INVENTION CONVENTION

Students participate in a convention, presenting inventions from specific Chinese dynasties.

MATERIALS

Invention Cards (page 16), scissors, reference books, Internet access, posterboard, markers

HERE'S HOW

1 Before beginning the activity, copy and cut out the four cards on *Invention Cards*.

2 Write these words on the board for students to see: *seismograph, fireworks, compass, gunpowder, paper, wheelbarrow, printing, cast iron, rockets, helicopter propeller,* and *matches*. Ask students what these items have in common. *(The Chinese invented them all.)*

3 Divide students into four groups. Assign each group to represent one of the following: Zhou Dynasty, Han Dynasty, Tang Dynasty, or Song Dynasty.

4 Distribute to groups their corresponding cards. Have groups read the information about their dynasties' inventions. (Point out to students that scholars sometimes disagree about the dates of certain inventions, so the cards may show dates that some scholars contest.) Allow groups to conduct research about their inventions, using reference books or the Internet.

5 Tell groups that they will act as representatives at an invention convention for the specific dynasty on their invention cards. Explain that each group will create a "booth" for the invention convention.

6 Have groups use posterboard and markers to create posters announcing their inventions, the dynasties they represent, and any other important information that the public needs to know.

7 Groups may also wish to create models or examples of their inventions.

8 Allow groups to present their "booths" to the class.

EXTENSION

Have groups find out about additional Chinese inventions and share their findings with the class.

INVENTION CARDS

Han Dynasty Representatives
(202 BC–8 AD; 25–220)

Paper: Paper was probably developed sometime between 202 BC and 16 AD. Early paper used bark from the hemp plant or mulberry tree. Cai Lin perfected the process in 105 by creating a smoother paper made from rope, rags, plant fiber, and fishing nets.

Seismograph: Zhang Heng invented the seismograph in the year 132. The seismograph, used to detect earthquakes, was a vessel with a pendulum and eight dragons holding bronze balls. When the earth moved, the pendulum moved, causing a ball to drop—indicating an earthquake and its direction.

Song Dynasty Representatives
(960–1279)

Rockets: Scientists are not sure when the Chinese invented rockets, but the first descriptions of their use appeared during the Song Dynasty. By this period, the Chinese were using gunpowder (invented during the Tang Dynasty) in weapons such as cannons and rockets. Rockets were also used for firework displays.

Moveable Type: In 1045, a printer named Bi Sheng invented moveable type. Each Chinese character was carved into a piece of clay, which was then baked. Words were arranged in an iron frame and then printed. The clay pieces were then removed and could be used again.

Zhou Dynasty Representatives
(1122 BC–256 BC)

Kite: Kites, the oldest type of aircraft, were probably invented in China during the fourth or fifth century BC. Kungshu P'an and Mo Ti were early kite makers who are mentioned in Chinese stories. Later, during the Han dynasty, the Chinese flew kites attached with whistling bamboo pipes to scare their enemies in battle.

Compass: The first compass was probably invented sometime between 480 BC and 221 BC. It consisted of a square bronze plate on which was placed a magnetized lodestone spoon, whose handle pointed south.

Tang Dynasty Representatives
(618–907)

Block Printing: In the seventh century, the Chinese printed with wooden blocks. This method of printing was extremely useful when reproducing the thousands of different Chinese characters.

Gunpowder: Gunpowder, made from potassium nitrate, sulfur, and carbon, was probably invented in the eighth or ninth century. Earlier, alchemists looking for the key to eternal life, experimented with substances that resulted in fires. Directions for flammable mixtures were recorded in books as early as the third century.

Ancient Civilizations: China, India, Africa, Mesopotamia   Scholastic Teaching Resources

THE CHINESE GAME OF GO

Students play the Chinese game of Go.

MATERIALS

Go Game Board (page 18), black and white beans or small game markers of two different colors

HERE'S HOW

1 Distribute a copy of *Go Game Board* to pairs of students. Gather enough game markers so that every pair has 81 of each color. Dried black and white beans work well. (See tip below for a math connection that puts students in charge of counting.)

2 Share with students the background information about Go on page 14. Tell pairs that, with a smaller game board, they will play a shorter version of this game of strategy.

3 Explain the following rules:

- The goal of the game is to gain more territory on the board than your opponent. Part of dominating the game board includes capturing your opponent. The player with the most territory wins.

- Black moves first. Players take turns placing their markers on an intersection created by the lines on the board. Markers can also be placed on the corners and edges of the board. Once a marker is placed on the board, it cannot be moved.

- A marker is captured when it is surrounded by the opponent's game pieces on all sides. When a marker is captured, it is removed from the board.

- Players may choose to place their markers next to each other in lines. However, entire lines of markers may also be captured when an opponent surrounds the line with his or her markers. Then the entire line of markers is removed from the board.

- Players may choose to pass rather than play. If both players pass in succession, the game ends. The game may also end when a player resigns, or both sides agree to end the game.

- To score, players count the number of empty intersections enclosed by their markers. They also count the number of intersections occupied by their markers. Players add these two numbers together to obtain a final score. The player with the higher score wins the game.

TIP

Make a math connection by having students count their markers from a bag or canister of beans, grouping by nines to gather 81.

Go Game Board

Ancient Civilizations: China, India, Africa, Mesopotamia   Scholastic Teaching Resources

CHINESE WRITING

Students write Chinese pictographs and calligraphy.

MATERIALS

Chinese Pictographs (page 20),
Writing Chinese Calligraphy (page 21),
paper, pencils, paintbrushes, paint

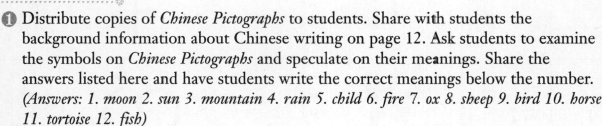

HERE'S HOW

1 Distribute copies of *Chinese Pictographs* to students. Share with students the background information about Chinese writing on page 12. Ask students to examine the symbols on *Chinese Pictographs* and speculate on their meanings. Share the answers listed here and have students write the correct meanings below the number. *(Answers: 1. moon 2. sun 3. mountain 4. rain 5. child 6. fire 7. ox 8. sheep 9. bird 10. horse 11. tortoise 12. fish)*

2 Have students draw these pictographs on a piece of paper. Explain that there are different ways to write both the pictographs and their corresponding modern characters. Point out that *Chinese Pictographs* shows only one way to write them.

3 Explain to students that calligraphy is the art of creating beautiful handwriting. Ask students if any of them have ever learned calligraphy. Explain to students that Chinese characters are written in calligraphy.

4 Distribute *Writing Chinese Calligraphy* to students. Again, emphasize that this page shows one of many ways to write Chinese characters. Guide students in forming Chinese characters using calligraphy. Let students use paint and paintbrushes to form their calligraphy on sheets of paper.

5 When students have finished writing their 12 words in calligraphy, arrange for them to visit other classrooms, partner with another student and teach their partners a short lesson about writing calligraphy. Students should be able to give a step-by-step demonstration for one or two characters and then offer tips and encouragement to their calligraphy "students."

CHINESE PICTOGRAPHS

The ancient Chinese used pictographs, or symbols that stood for a word or idea. Chinese pictographs later developed into characters, or written symbols. See how the pictographs below developed into the characters used today.

	Ancient	Modern		Ancient	Modern
1. _____	月	月	7. _____	牛	牛
2. _____	日	日	8. _____	羊	羊
3. _____	山	山	9. _____	鳥	鳥
4. _____	雨	雨	10. _____	馬	馬
5. _____	子	子	11. _____	龜	龜
6. _____	火	火	12. _____	魚	魚

Ancient Civilizations: China, India, Africa, Mesopotamia Scholastic Teaching Resources

WRITING CHINESE CALLIGRAPHY

To write Chinese calligraphy, the basic strokes generally go in a certain direction. For example, vertical lines, angles, and curves always start at the top and go down. Horizontal lines, angles, and curves go from left to right.

There is one exception for a stroke that is written from right to left.

Practice writing these characters on a sheet of paper using paint and paintbrushes. Keep your wrist and elbow raised.

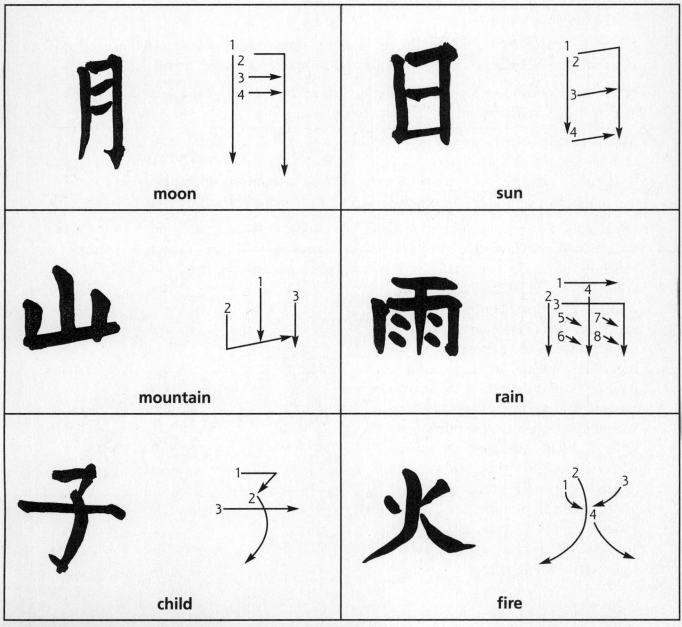

moon

sun

mountain

rain

child

fire

MULAN: CAMPAIGNING FOR A WARRIOR

Students conduct research about Mulan and create a book about her.

MATERIALS

Internet access, reference books, paper, pencils, pens, colored pencils or markers, stapler

HERE'S HOW

1. Share with students the background information about Mulan on page 14. Ask students whether they think that Mulan, an ancient Chinese heroine, is a real person or a fictional character.

2. Encourage students to read the English version of the *Ballad of Mulan* in books or on Web sites such as **http://utd500.utdallas.edu/~hairston/mulan.html**.

3. Have students conduct a poll throughout their school to see what others know about Mulan. Have students report their findings.

4. Ask students to conduct research about Mulan to determine whether or not she was a real person or a fictional character. Have students gather research by examining reference books and Web sites such as **http://www.chinavista.com/travel/mulan/part2.html**, which describes a reporter's visit to Mulan's hometown in Henan Province.

5. Once students have read the information, divide the class into two groups for a school-wide campaign. Have one group campaign in support of Mulan's existence. This group will run on the platform that Mulan was an actual person who lived and fought in her father's place. Have the other group campaign to dissuade others of Mulan's existence. (It is important to assign these positions to your students regardless of what they personally believe; having them find the strongest argument in defense of contrasting viewpoints helps them to think critically.) This campaign can include posters, speeches (to be held in the cafeteria during lunch or over the loud speaker during the day), a 10-minute mini-debate, and a final vote cast by the class, a grade level, or even the whole school.

GOVERNMENT AND RELIGION

The Terra Cotta Army

The first emperor to unite all of China was Shi Huangdi, who ruled from 221 BC to 210 BC. In addition to the work that he ordered on the Great Wall, Shi Huangdi created a single system of writing and money. When this emperor died, he arranged to have a secret buried with him: a clay army consisting of more than 7,500 men, horses, and chariots made from terra cotta—a type of baked clay. The terra cotta army was buried near the emperor's tomb as if protecting it in the afterlife. It was accidentally unearthed in 1974 by well diggers. Each statue is life-size and weighs hundreds of pounds. There are infantry, cavalry, and officers among the terra cotta figures, which are organized into specific formations as if marching into battle. Solders have unique faces and wear specific uniforms that identify their rank.

Chinese Silk

According to one Chinese legend, the wife of Emperor Huangdi developed a method for weaving silk sometime around 2700 BC. Chinese emperors were clothed in silk robes containing elaborately embroidered symbols, such as the dragon—which was a symbol of the emperor and imperial power. Depending on the dynasty and time period, the embroidery on these silk robes varied. Although silk material was exported to various places along the Mediterranean Sea, the Chinese kept the secret of making silk. China traded silk with Persia, who then sold the silk at a high cost in the Roman Empire. Tired of paying high prices for silk, the Roman emperor sent two monks to China in the year 550. These two monks smuggled silkworms and mulberry seeds out of China—and revealed the secret of making silk to the world.

Chinese Religions

Confucianism and Taoism are both philosophies as well as religions. Confucianism developed from the teachings of Confucius, who lived from 551 BC to 479 BC. These teachings stress the way to virtue through strong ethics, respect for authority figures, close family ties, and the practice of tradition and ritual. Among the rituals that Confucius advocated were ancestor worship. Laozi, who was probably born in 604 BC and died in 531 BC, was an early proponent of Taoism—which stresses that people should live simply and in harmony with nature. Taoists disapproved of Confucius's prescription for organizing and regulating society because it represented an aggressive attempt to control other people. Taoists practice kindness, tolerance, and quiet contemplation. Refusal to partake in aggressive behavior is stressed. Some Taoists seek immortality through various means, such as magic and alchemy. By the end of the first century, Buddhism—founded in India about 2,500 years ago by Siddhartha Gautama—was introduced to China. From the 300s to the 500s, Buddhism challenged Confucianism and Taoism as a popular religion. Buddhists strived to free themselves of earthly desires and suffering by reaching nirvana—a state of happiness and peace.

CRAFTING TERRA COTTA SOLDIERS

Students craft replicas of terra cotta soldiers and create a class museum of their army.

MATERIALS

Pictures of the Terra Cotta Army (page 25), reference books, Internet access, self-hardening dough or clay, paint, brushes, paper, pens, index cards

HERE'S HOW

© David Nemelka

❶ Distribute *Pictures of the Terra Cotta Army* to students and direct them to look at the illustrations. Ask students what they think the pictures show. Then share the background information about the terra cotta army on page 23.

❷ Have students conduct research about the terra cotta army using reference books, such as Jane O'Connor's *The Emperor's Silent Army*, or the Internet.

❸ Tell students that they will make a terra cotta army for a classroom museum. Students may choose to create archers, charioteers, generals, infantrymen, cavalrymen, or horses. Have students create four-inch-tall figures using dough or clay.

❹ Allow figures to harden overnight. Then let students paint their figures. Ask students to create labels that provide information about their figures. To make a stand-up label for the figurines, use folded index cards. Have each student fold an index card so that it stands in an upside down V on its own. Students can write on one side of their cards, listing the figure's rank, gear, weapons, and any other notable features. Have them stand these cards beside their figurines.

❺ Have students create a museum exhibit in which they display their army in formation.

EXTENSION

Let students give tours of their museum exhibit to other classes.

Pictures of the Terra Cotta Army

© David Nemelka   © David Nemelka

© David Nemelka

DESIGNING AN EMPEROR'S SILK ROBES

Students design an emperor's silk robe that tells the story of how silk was spread to the world.

MATERIALS

reference books; Internet access; paper; pencils; crayons, markers or colored pencils

HERE'S HOW

1. Share with students the background information about silk on page 23. Direct students to look at reference books and the Internet for more information about Chinese robes. Students can learn about different Chinese symbols on robes at such Internet sites as **http://dept.kent.edu/museum/project/Erin/symbol1.htm**.

2. Tell students that they have been commissioned by the emperor to design a silk robe that tells how the secret of making silk spread throughout the world. Encourage students to research how the secret of silk escaped from China, using reference materials or the Internet.

3. Have students draw a robe on a plain sheet of paper. You may wish to create a transparency of the robe on this page to show students on an overhead projector. They can use this model as a guide. Have students use crayons, colored pencils, or markers to design their robes.

4. After students complete their designs, display the silk robes on a bulletin board with a student created summary or time line tracing the history of silk.

COMPARING CHINESE RELIGIONS

Students identify aspects of Confucianism, Taoism, and Buddhism.

MATERIALS

reference books, Internet access, *Confucianism and Taoism* (page 28), paper, pencils

HERE'S HOW

1. Share with students the background information about Chinese religions on page 23.

2. Have small groups of students research Confucianism and Taoism using reference books and the Internet. Invite groups to discuss these religions.

3. Distribute to each group a copy of *Confucianism and Taoism*. Tell students that both Confucianism and Taoism are religions that developed in China. Direct students to look at the illustration of the yin and yang symbol. Explain that this is an ancient Chinese concept that was embraced by Taoists.

4. Have groups work together to complete the worksheet. If groups have difficulty completing the worksheet, allow them to conduct further research.

5. Encourage groups to research Buddhism, which arrived in China during the first century. Have groups create a three-oval Venn diagram that compares Buddhism, Confucianism, and Taoism like the one below. To simplify the activity, have students create a traditional Venn diagram that compares only two of these religions.

EXTENSION

Have groups create a worksheet similar to *Confucianism and Taoism*. Direct groups to include scenarios on their worksheets that a Buddhist, Confucianist, or Taoist would follow. Have groups exchange their worksheets with another group and identify each other's scenarios.

Answers for page 28

1. Confucianism
2. Taoism
3. Confucianism
4. Confucianism
5. Taoism
6. Confucianism
7. Confucianism
8. Taoism

Students' Venn diagrams will vary. The diagram to the right is one possible model.

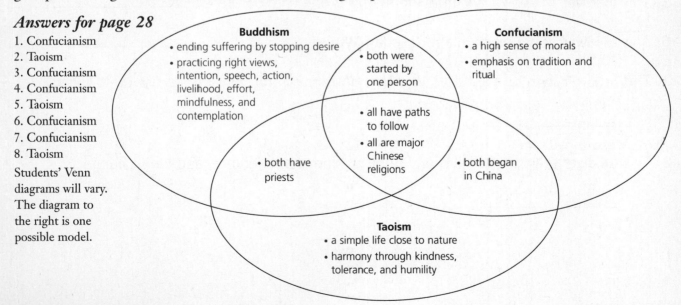

Buddhism
• ending suffering by stopping desire
• practicing right views, intention, speech, action, livelihood, effort, mindfulness, and contemplation

Confucianism
• a high sense of morals
• emphasis on tradition and ritual

• both were started by one person

• all have paths to follow
• all are major Chinese religions

• both have priests

• both began in China

Taoism
• a simple life close to nature
• harmony through kindness, tolerance, and humility

CONFUCIANISM AND TAOISM

The Yin and Yang represent opposite forces in traditional Chinese thought, as well as in Taoism. The Yin is the shaded area that represents receptivity and darkness. The Yang is the white area that represents activity and brightness. The Yin and Yang are thought by Taoists to be the building blocks of the universe— both opposing and complementary forces that are in constant fluctuation.

Read the statements below. Decide whether each statement supports the beliefs of Confucianism or Taoism. Write "Confucianism" or "Taoism" on the line.

1. The follower must be disciplined with a high sense of morals. _____

2. Some followers strive to gain immortality. _____

3. This follower places an emphasis on traditions and rituals. _____

4. This follower respects authority figures. _____

5. This follower strives for a simple life that is at one with nature. _____

6. This follower hopes to maintain close family ties. _____

7. This follower lives by the rule, "What you do not wish for yourself, do not do to others."

_____

8. This follower searches for harmony through kindness, tolerance, and being humble.

_____

INDIA
Map and Time Line

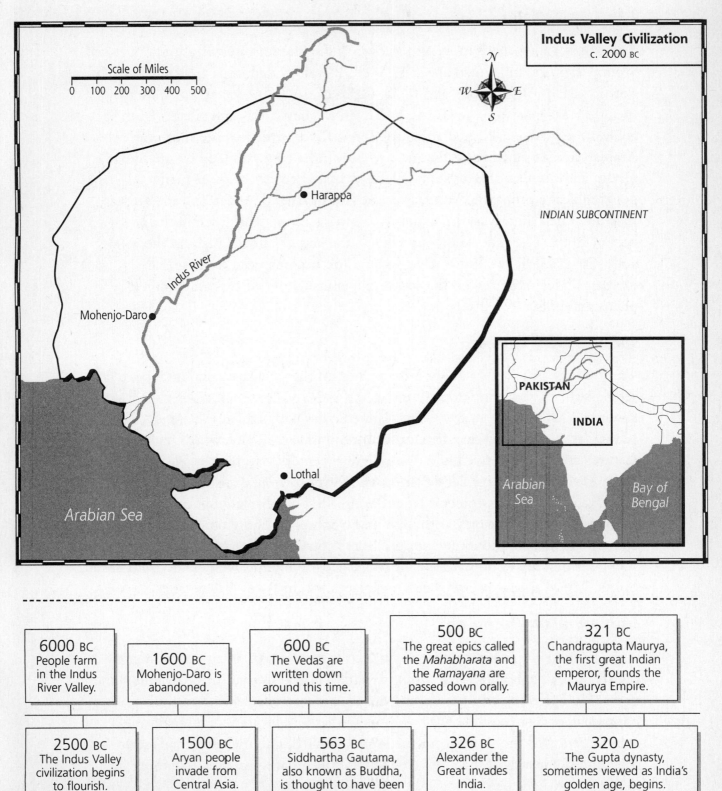

Scale of Miles
0 100 200 300 400 500

Indus Valley Civilization
c. 2000 BC

N W E S

Harappa

INDIAN SUBCONTINENT

Indus River

Mohenjo-Daro

PAKISTAN

INDIA

Lothal

Arabian Sea

Arabian Sea

Bay of Bengal

6000 BC
People farm in the Indus River Valley.

1600 BC
Mohenjo-Daro is abandoned.

600 BC
The Vedas are written down around this time.

500 BC
The great epics called the *Mahabharata* and the *Ramayana* are passed down orally.

321 BC
Chandragupta Maurya, the first great Indian emperor, founds the Maurya Empire.

2500 BC
The Indus Valley civilization begins to flourish.

1500 BC
Aryan people invade from Central Asia.

563 BC
Siddhartha Gautama, also known as Buddha, is thought to have been born on this date.

326 BC
Alexander the Great invades India.

320 AD
The Gupta dynasty, sometimes viewed as India's golden age, begins.

Geography and Architecture

Land and Water

The Indus Valley civilization, also known as the Harappan civilization, flourished around 2500 BC and ended about 1700 BC. It was located in parts of what are now Pakistan, Afghanistan, and India. Cities of the Indus Valley civilization include Harappa, Mohenjo-Daro, and Lothal. Many cities and villages of this civilization were established along the Indus River, which empties into the Arabian Sea. In addition to the Arabian Sea, India is surrounded by the Indian Ocean and the Bay of Bengal. The land of India consists of three main geographical regions: the Himalayas, the Indo-Gangetic Plain, and the Deccan Plateau. The Himalayas, the highest mountains in the world, are in the northern part of India. The Indo-Gangetic Plain is the largest alluvial plain in the world and is irrigated by the Indus, Ganges, and the Brahmaputra Rivers. The Deccan Plateau, located on the southern peninsula of India, is a mixture of plains and hills.

Indus Valley Cities

The ruins of two ancient Indus Valley cities, Mohenjo-Daro and Harappa, tell scholars much about urban planning in the Indus Valley. Both cities, which were about one square mile in size, were planned cities with similar rectangular layouts. Indus Valley cities had two distinct sections: a walled citadel, which included such features as administrative buildings, religious centers, bathhouses, and granaries; and a lower town, or residential area. The lower town may also have been protected by walls to protect it from floods. Streets were laid out in grids that formed blocks with homes. Although many homes had only one room, others contained multiple rooms and stories. Some contained inner courtyards and brick staircases that led to upper floors or roofs. Most buildings were made from baked bricks. There appear to have been no palaces within Indus Valley cities.

Indus Valley Plumbing

The Indus Valley civilization was advanced in many ways, including residential plumbing. Some homes were equipped with bathrooms that included toilets and baths. Houses received their water from their own wells, located in the home's courtyard, or from a public well. A drainage system, located underneath the streets, removed the water from the homes. This plumbing system helped to maintain the health of the cities' residents. Public bathhouses, and bathing in general, may have been associated with religious rituals.

INDUS VALLEY TRAVEL AGENTS

Students plot a map for a tour of ancient Indus Valley sites.

MATERIALS

Indus Valley Travel Map (page 32), colored pencils, reference materials, Internet access

HERE'S HOW

❶ Tell students that they are travel agents who specialize in tours of mysterious and ancient places. Explain to students that a client has contacted them to book a trip to ancient Indus Valley sites. Students must provide a map for this client and explain the best places to visit.

❷ Share with students the background information on page 30 about India's land and water and Indus Valley cities.

❸ Distribute to students *Indus Valley Travel Map*. Have them follow the instructions to create a map for their clients. Allow students to use reference materials and Web sites to fill in their maps.

Answers

Students descriptions will vary, but may include— Harappa: an ancient Indus Valley city on the Indus River in what is now Pakistan; Kalibangan: an ancient Indus Valley city on the now extinct Ghaggar-Hakra River in what is now India; Lothal: a small Indus Valley settlement near the Sabarmati River and the Arabian Sea in what is now India; Mohenjo-Daro: an ancient Indus Valley city on the Indus River in what is now Pakistan; Rupar: an ancient Indus Valley city on the Sutlej River in what is now India; Himalaya Mountains: the world's highest mountain system located in India and Tibet; Indo-Gangetic Plain: the world's largest alluvial plain; Deccan Plateau: a plateau on the southern peninsula of India; Indus River: the longest river in Pakistan and a source for one of the world's largest irrigation systems; Ganges River: one of the world's longest rivers, considered sacred by Hindus, and located in India and Bangladesh; Brahmaputra River: an important waterway that flows from the Himalaya Mountains in Tibet to the Ganges River in India; Arabian Sea: a northern part of the Indian Ocean.

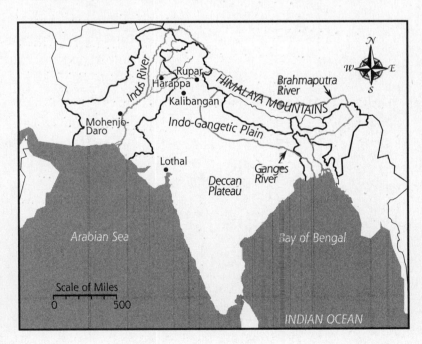

Name _____   Date _____

INDUS VALLEY TRAVEL MAP

You are a travel agent. A client asks you to book a trip of ancient Indus Valley sites. Use the map below to show your client famous Indus Valley sites as well as major geographical features of the region.

Your client wants to see how people lived in the Indus Valley civilization. On the map, show your client where these famous archaeological sites are located: Harappa, Kalibangan, Lothal, Mohenjo-Daro, and Rupar.

Your client might also want to visit some of the natural regions near the Indus Valley civilization. On the map, show your client where these areas are located: the Himalaya Mountains, Indo-Gangetic Plain, Deccan Plateau, Brahmaputra River, Ganges River, Indus River, the Arabian Sea.

So that your client knows some background information on these cities and geographical features, provide a brief description on the back of this page.

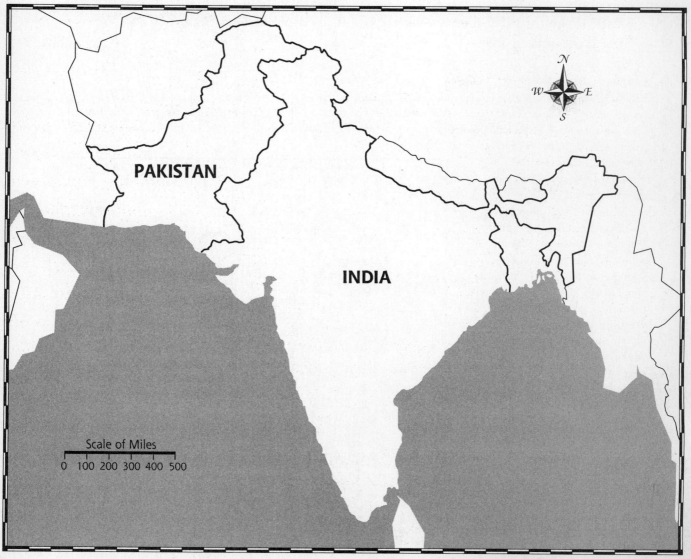

DESIGNING AN INDUS VALLEY CITY

Students design and build a model city in the Indus Valley.

MATERIALS

Ancient Urban Planning (page 34), Internet access, graph paper, pencils, colored pencils, recycled materials (such as small boxes) for building, construction paper, glue, scissors, tape, markers

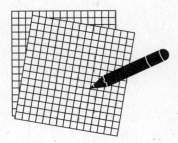

HERE'S HOW

1. Divide the class into small groups of two to four students. Share the background information on page 30 about Indus Valley cities and plumbing.

2. Tell groups that they are architects and their architectural firms will compete in a contest to build a new Indus Valley city for the growing Indus Valley population. Their firms must design, name, and build a model of their proposed new city.

3. Distribute copies of *Ancient Urban Planning* to each group. Have groups answer the questions. Then direct groups to assign group members different sections of the city to design. Have students record the assignments on their worksheets. For example, in a group of five, two students might work on the residential section of the city, another student could design the citadel area with help from two other students who are responsible for the Great Bath and the granary.

4. Have groups design their new city on graph paper. (Each group member should design his or her assigned city section on a separate piece of graph paper.) Students may wish to search the Internet for ideas. For example there is a city map of Mohenjo-Daro at **www.mnsu.edu/emuseum/archaeology/sites/middle_east/mohenjo_daro.html**.

5. When the designs are complete, have students tape their graph papers together to form the city plan.

6. Have groups build a model of a section of their proposed city using recycled materials, such as small boxes. Students may wish to show roads by cutting out strips of construction paper. Tell groups to use a colored pencil to shade the city section that the model represents on their graph paper.

7. Have groups display their designs and models. Allow the class to vote for the best design. The best design can be chosen based on the criteria students have discovered in their research, including an upper and lower section of the city, a great wall, wide straight roads with right angles, neatly rowed houses, and so on.

ANCIENT URBAN PLANNING

Your architectural firm has been asked to participate in a competition to plan a new Indus Valley city for the growing population. Answer the questions below.

What is the name of your architectural firm? _____

Who are the members of your architectural firm? _____

_____

What is the proposed name for your town? _____

Some ancient Indus Valley cities could house up to 40,000 people. About how many people

could live in your city at full capacity? _____

As you plan your city, don't forget to include the following: the walled citadel with administrative and public buildings—such as a bath and granary; a lower town, or residential section with homes; and roads. Use graph paper to show detailed sections of your city. Each member of your firm should work on a different section of the city. Below, list each firm member's name and the section that he or she will design. When your firm's work is complete, tape the graph paper together to show the city in its entirety.

Firm member:	Responsible for:

Ancient Civilizations: China, India, Africa, Mesopotamia Scholastic Teaching Resources

HELP WANTED: INDUS VALLEY PLUMBERS

Students write a help-wanted advertisement for an Indus Valley plumber.

MATERIALS

reference books, Internet access, paper, pens, colored markers

HERE'S HOW

1. Ask students to brainstorm what life might be like without plumbing. Write students' ideas on the board.

2. Share with students the background information about Indus Valley plumbing on page 30.

3. Have students conduct further research on Indus Valley plumbing, using reference books and Web sites such as **http://www.sewerhistory.org/grfx/wh_region/indus1.htm**.

4. Tell students that they will create a help-wanted advertisement for plumbers in the Indus Valley civilization. (Have on hand several examples from the classified section of help-wanted ads for students to use as models.) Remind students to use what they have learned about Indus Valley plumbing to formulate their advertisements.

5. Once the advertisements are complete, display the help-wanted ads on a bulletin board.

Indus Valley Seals

Indus Valley seals, which usually featured pictographs and a picture of an animal, were used for identification in business dealings. They have been found in Mesopotamia, indicating that they were used in trade. These small seals were imprinted on ceramics and clay tags that were attached to goods. They were used to seal items for security reasons or to show ownership. They were typically square and cut from steatite, a soft stone. Many of the seals were fired and glazed to make them durable. Seals had a perforated back to hang them on cords, which could be worn around the neck. The engraved pictures of animals on seals included antelope, elephants, rhinoceros, tigers, water buffalo, and mythical creatures. The unicorn with a trough is depicted on many seals. Some scholars believe that the animal is not a unicorn, but rather a sacred bull shown in profile with one horn. The unicorn's trough has many interpretations among scholars, including an incense burner, a manger, and an offering stand.

Indus Valley Pictographs

Pictographs are symbols that represent objects rather than sounds. Over 400 different Indus Valley pictographs have been discovered. However, because Indus Valley pottery and seals have only five or six pictographs each, it is difficult for scholars to decipher the meanings of the symbols. Scholars hope that a bilingual tablet containing both Indus Valley pictographs and a duplicate text, such as Sanskrit or another known language, will one day be found. Some scholars believe that Indus Valley people may have written longer texts on cloth or palm leaves, which have since disintegrated.

The Ramayana

Ancient India is known for two classical epics: the *Ramayana* and the *Mahabharata*. Both epics incorporate Hindu deities. Passed down orally from generation to generation, the *Ramayana* and the *Mahabharata* are thought to have first been written down around 300 BC—after the disappearance of the Indus Valley civilization. The *Ramayana* tells the story of a prince named Rama, who is a human form of the Hindu god Vishnu. Rama is exiled from his father's kingdom, and soon after, a demon kidnaps Rama's wife, Sita. This epic tale embodies lessons in loyalty, devotion, and the triumph of good over evil.

A Civilization's End

The Indus Valley civilization gradually began to disappear around 1700 BC. This disappearance may have been caused by a natural catastrophe along with an invasion. Most archaeologists believe that the Indus Valley people moved south because of a natural catastrophe that resulted in the ruin of their economy.

Designing an Indus Valley Seal

Students create Indus Valley seals.

Materials

overhead transparency (optional), overhead projector (optional), reference books, Internet access, paper, pencils, self-hardening clay, carving instruments such as rounded-tip toothpicks

Here's How

1. If possible, create a transparency of the Indus Valley unicorn seal on this page to show to students on an overhead projector. Or have students view a unicorn seal on the Internet at such sites as **http:www.metmuseum.org/explore/First_Cities/seals_indus.htm**. Ask students to speculate on how they think this object was used in ancient India.

2. Share with students the background information about Indus Valley seals on page 36. Have students conduct further research about Indus Valley seals, using reference books and the Internet.

3. Have students create on paper a design for a seal of ownership.

4. Instruct students to create their own Indus Valley–style seals out of clay. Have students take a small lump of self-hardening clay that is about the size of their thumbs. Direct students to form the clay into a square shape. Let students use toothpicks, or other appropriate carving instruments, to make their designs. Students can create a hole at the top of their seal, away from the design so they can hang it by a string or cord when it has dried.

5. When the clay has hardened, after about 24 hours, have students use their seals to stamp their signs. To do this, give each student another small piece of clay. Direct students to place the clay on a piece of paper. Have them flatten the clay into a rectangular shape, then roll their seals over the clay to make imprints. Have them gently pick up the clay piece, inscribe their initials on the back with a toothpick, and let it dry on the paper. When the clay pieces have dried, collect them in a basket or box. You might use these as a visual cue to call on a student or select a student for an activity: Select a marked clay piece from the basket and hold it up for the class to see. The student whose mark is shown is selected.

DECIPHERING INDUS VALLEY PICTOGRAPHS

Students decipher five Indus Valley pictographs.

MATERIALS

Indus Valley Dictionary (page 39), paper, pens or pencils, stapler

HERE'S HOW

1 Share with students the background information about Indus Valley pictographs on page 36.

2 Distribute copies of *Indus Valley Dictionary* to students. Tell students that an Indus dictionary does not exist because scholars have been unable to decode the language.

3 Divide the class into small groups. Tell each group that they will create an Indus Valley dictionary. Instruct each group to define five signs shown on *Indus Valley Dictionary*. Tell groups to put each sign and its definition on a separate piece of paper. Instruct groups to provide a written reason for each sign's definition. Have groups staple their pages together to form a book.

4 After the dictionaries are completed, have groups present them to the class.

5 Encourage a friendly debate among the amateur "scholars" about the meanings of the pictographs. Explain to students that disagreements are a common occurrence among scholars. Share some of the theories scholars have come up with below.

Answers

Accept all suggestions from students. Scholars have theorized the following possibilities:

Ʊ the head of a cow, a jar, or a vessel that stands for a priest

↑ a lance or spear that stands for a warrior

⚘ a bearer that stands for an official

⚘ a combination of the jar and bearer that stands for a priestly official

⚘ a combination of the lance and bearer that stands for a military officer

𓀂 a person that stands for a person or servant

⚶ a fish that stands for a fish or star

⚶ fish with dot that stands for a carp, a star, or a red dot

⏀⏀ rings that stand for a boy or youth

E a harrow, a type of farm equipment, that stands for a farmer or tenant

INDUS VALLEY DICTIONARY

Your team of scholars must create an Indus Valley dictionary. Working as a team, choose five pictographs from this page to include in your dictionary. Draw and define each pictograph on a separate piece of paper. Then, write an explanation for each definition on the page.

Of the approximately 400 signs that archaeologists have found, there are five signs that occur very often.

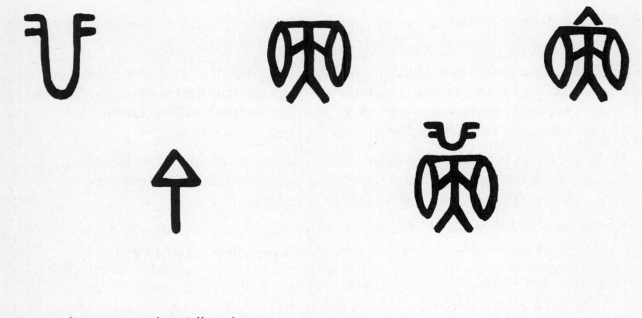

Here are five more Indus Valley signs.

The Ramayana: A Movie

Students read a version of the Ramayana *and cast a movie version of the epic.*

MATERIALS

Internet access, *Casting the Ramayana* (page 41), posterboard, pencils, markers

HERE'S HOW

1. Ask students to define an epic. Create an idea web on the board, using students' definitions. Explain that an epic is usually a long poem about a hero.

2. Ask students if they have heard of an ancient epic titled the *Ramayana*. Have students read a comic-book version or a simple version of the epic on such Web sites as **http://www.askasia.org/adult_free_zone/virtual_gallery/exhibitions/index.htm** and **http://www.boloji.com/hinduism/ramayana/**.

3. Group students in pairs. Distribute to each pair a copy of *Casting the Ramayana*. Ask pairs to read the instructions. Point out to students that the *Ramayana* contains many more roles than they have been hired to cast.

4. Tell pairs that they may choose to cast movie stars, celebrities, or other people they know in the film. Explain that when casting a role, students should chose the performer who best fits the part in appearance and temperament. Allow pairs to conduct further research on the Internet to find out more about each role. For each character on the casting sheet, have students write the name of the chosen actor and list the actor's traits that best match the character he or she will portray.

5. After pairs have completed their casting, ask them to create posters with the name of their film and the performers who will star in their movie. Display these coming attractions around the classroom.

CASTING THE RAMAYANA

You have been hired by a Hollywood producer to cast a film version of the *Ramayana*. Write the names of the performers who you think should play the following roles. Then write the characteristics that make them perfect for this role. Remember that the star of the epic is Rama.

Dasaratha: King of Ayodhya and father of Rama

_____ _____
(actor)   (characteristics)

Kausalya: King Dasaratha's principal wife and Rama's mother

_____ _____

Rama: King Dasaratha and Kausalya's son and an incarnation of the god Vishnu

_____ _____

Vishwamitra: a great sage

_____ _____

Janaka: King of Mithila and father of Sita

_____ _____

Sita: daughter of King Janaka, the incarnation of the goddess Lakshmi, and Rama's wife

_____ _____

Surpanakha: a demon woman and sister of Ravana

_____ _____

Ravana: 10-headed demon King of Lanka and brother of Surpanakha

_____ _____

Sugriva: the Monkey King

_____ _____

Hanuman: part monkey and part man, son of the wind god Vayu

_____ _____

SKETCHING A CIVILIZATION'S DISAPPEARANCE

Students sketch the effects of possible causes of the Indus Valley civilization's disappearance.

MATERIALS

overhead transparencies, overhead markers, overhead projector

HERE'S HOW

1 Share the background information on page 36 about the disappearance of the Indus Valley civilization. Tell students that scholars debate this topic and have developed a number of theories to explain the mysterious disappearance.

2 Divide the class into groups of three. Distribute overhead transparencies and overhead markers to students.

3 Write the following causes on the board: *climate changes, drought, floods, erosion, change in the Indus River's path, drying up of other rivers, earthquakes,* and *invaders*.

4 Have groups select one or two causes and sketch pictures on their transparencies that show how these causes might have contributed to the disappearance of the Indus Valley civilization. For example, groups might sketch a picture of a field with dying plants to show drought, or a picture of a family moving from a flooding river.

5 When students have finished their drawings, have them share their overhead transparencies with the class.

6 Encourage friendly debate among students as they present their scenarios. Explain that debates are a common occurrence among scholars. Help students to realize that these causes would have affected agriculture and the economy of the Indus Valley.

GOVERNMENT AND RELIGION

The Vedic Caste System

The Vedic period dates from the Aryan invasion of about 1500 BC. The Aryans migrated from central Asia to the Indus Valley and other places in India. They brought with them many aspects of their culture, including hymns about how the world operates. Around 600 BC, these hymns—which were a foundation for Hinduism—were collected into books called Vedas. The Vedas included a hymn that was the basis for India's caste system, which labels a person's rank in society by birth. Although there are thousands of different castes in India today, Aryan leaders determined four main categories based on varnas, or colors. They were: Brahmans or priests, which were white; Kshatriyas or warriors and rulers, which were red; Vaisyas or merchants and traders, which were yellow; and Sudras or workers and servants, which were black. The panchamas, or outcasts, were another group in society who were not allowed to dwell among the other castes. People usually did not marry or associate with others outside of their caste. According to belief, people could climb up the caste system only in another life.

Chandragupta

Born into poverty in the early 300s BC, Chandragupta became the first Indian emperor to unify most of India. As a boy, Chandragupta was sold to a Brahman politician and received a military education. He met Alexander the Great and set his sights on advancement. After the death of Alexander the Great in 323 BC, Chandragupta was able to take control of much of India. Around 321 BC, he became ruler of the Maura Empire. He expanded the empire and improved roads and canals. Although he taxed and punished people harshly, his empire prospered economically. To ensure that he was obeyed, Chandragupta created a network of spies throughout his kingdom who reported to him. Chandragupta probably died in 297 BC.

Religion

Two ancient religions of India are Hinduism and Buddhism. Hinduism, which is the main religion of India, developed from different cultures and religions. Among its many sacred writings are four books called the Vedas, whose teachings were passed down orally before being recorded around 600 BC. Hinduism includes many gods, although some Hindus believe that the gods are all forms of one spirit called Brahman. The most important gods are Brahma, the creator; Vishnu, the preserver; and Shiva, the destroyer. Hinduism includes the concepts of dharma, or laws and duties; reincarnation, or rebirth; and karma, or a force generated by good or bad actions that influence reincarnation. Like Hinduism, Buddhism includes the ideas of dharma, karma, and reincarnation. Siddhartha Gautama, or Buddha, was born around 563 BC near the Himalayas. Although he was born into a wealthy family, the poverty of others impacted his life. He became a monk and traveled for six years until he received enlightenment. He spent the rest of his life teaching. His central message involved the elimination of suffering through the removal of desire in order to reach a state of bliss called nirvana.

A Vedic Caste System Simulation

Students participate in a simulation of the Vedic caste system.

MATERIALS

Caste Cards (page 45), scissors, tape, paper cups, paper, pencils or pens

HERE'S HOW

1. Create multiple copies and cut out *Caste Cards*.

2. As students come into class, randomly distribute a card with a caste name to each student. The caste names are: Brahman, Kshatriya, Vaisya, and Sudra. Have students tape their cards to their clothing.

3. Seat students according to the designations on their caste cards. Seat the Brahmans (priests) in the best seats, the Kshatriyas (warriors) in the next best seats, the Vaisyas (merchants) in the worst seats, and the Sudras (servants) on the floor. Inform the class that the outcasts are not allowed to come into class. (No students are chosen for this caste.)

4. Tell students that they will receive instructions throughout the day that apply to their castes. Explain that some instructions require them to consult with other members of their caste.

5. Throughout the day or class period, periodically distribute to students *Caste Cards* that correspond with their assigned castes. Allow time for students to complete the activities.

6. During all the activities, make sure the differential treatment is obvious and in accordance with each caste. Do not provide students with any explanation for the treatment. Do make sure that students assign or perform tasks that are appropriate for the classroom.

7. As the class period or day comes to an end, ask students whether they enjoyed being a part of a caste system. Ask students to discuss what they have learned about their castes from their cards and the way that others treated them. Then, share with students the background information about the Vedic caste system on page 43.

CASTE CARDS

❋ BRAHMAN ❋	❋ KSHATRIYA ❋	❋ VAISYA ❋	❋ SUDRA ❋
Since your caste spends so much time meditating and studying rituals, your caste may eliminate two questions or problems on any assignment today.	You have just returned from battle and are tired and thirsty. Ask members of the Vaisya caste or the Sudra caste to get you a glass of water.	Think of a gift that you can offer to the Brahmans. Make a formal presentation to the Brahmans in front of the other castes.	Present yourself to the Brahmans. Offer any service they need and perform it gladly.
Your leadership is well respected. With the other Brahmans (and your teacher), decide on an activity for other castes to do. Make sure that the activity is done correctly.	You have had a hard day in the world of politics. You may eliminate one question or problem from your homework today.	You suspect that some of your cattle have been stolen. You must consult the Kshatriyas to bring the guilty to justice. Write a summary about the incident and present it to the Kshatriyas.	Present yourself to the Kshatriyas. Offer any service they need and perform it gladly.
Create a new set of classroom rules for the other castes. Present them to the teacher.	Think of a gift that you can offer to the Brahmans. Make a formal presentation to the Brahmans in front of the other castes.	Your trading business has grown and you are feeling overwhelmed. Prepare a ledger showing all the transactions that have taken place in the past day.	Present yourself to the Vaisyas. Offer any service they need and perform it gladly.
You are entitled to donations from every other caste. Decide on something that each caste can donate to you and collect it.	You have heard rumors that the Vaisya and Sudra castes have not obeyed class rules. Think of a punishment for them and make an informative speech to the class.	Your business has expanded and you need help. Create a help-wanted advertisement.	Think of a gift that you can offer to the Brahmans. Make a formal presentation to the Brahmans in front of the other castes.

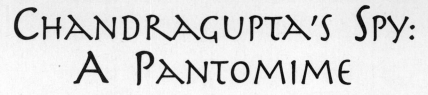

CHANDRAGUPTA'S SPY: A PANTOMIME

Students enact a story about a journey to serve Chandragupta.

MATERIALS

paper, pens

HERE'S HOW

❶ Tell students that as you read the following story, they will silently act it out. Clear enough space in the classroom so that students can move around.

❷ Read the following scenario to the class:

It is the year 310 BC. You have been summoned to appear before Chandragupta, the first emperor of India. It has been a long journey to the capital city, Pataliputra, which is in northeast India near the Ganges River. As you approach the city, you carefully slide off your elephant and give him a gentle pat on the side. You see directly in front of you a moat, which is hundreds of feet wide and surrounds the city. You look up and are relieved to see a small boat that can take you across. You carefully wade into the water and climb into the boat. You look around for some oars and see that they are in the bottom of the boat. You use the oars to paddle the boat to the other side. You don't want to fall into this moat because it's very deep! When you reach the city you climb out, thankful for the ground under your feet. You find that you are in the wealthy part of town. The homes have the most beautiful flowers you have ever seen! You stop to smell them and pick a piece of fruit hanging from a tree to take with you. You are amazed at all the sights: the university, a horse race track, the archery competition, and more. You love Chandragupta's capital! Speaking of Chandragupta, you've heard much about him. He's chosen you to join his secret service. Your resumé speaks for itself. You are honest, smart, and most important, you are related to one of Chandragupta's most trusted generals. As you walk toward Chandragupta's palace, you ponder the type of job you may be assigned. You imagine that you are his food tester. You bring the goblet up to your mouth and take a long drink. It might take only a few seconds to see if it is poisoned before you fall to the ground dead. You hope you don't get that job. Think of another possibility! You might be an assassin. You imagine that Chandragupta hands you a scroll, which you unroll. The orders tell you who needs to disappear for a while—or forever. That doesn't sound too appealing, either. You might have to disguise yourself as a merchant, prisoner, acrobat, or snake charmer to get secret information for Chandragupta. You know that he has spies throughout the kingdom. Oh, well—you are ready for your assignment.

❸ After you finish reading, have students write about their life in Chandragupta's secret service, as a diary entry, focusing on one exciting day.

❹ Combine students' tales into a spy magazine for others to read.

TEACHINGS OF BUDDHISM AND HINDUISM

Students create an illustrated guide to two Indian religions.

MATERIALS

A Guide to Buddhism and Hinduism (page 48), paper, pencils and pens, colored pencils or markers, hole punch, yarn

HERE'S HOW

1. Share with students the background information about Indian religions on page 43.

2. Divide the class into groups of four. Tell groups that they will create illustrated guides to Buddhism or Hinduism. Divide groups so that half of the groups illustrate Buddhism and the other half illustrate Hinduism.

3. Distribute to each group one copy of *A Guide to Buddhism and Hinduism*. Point out that there are four entries under both Buddhism and Hinduism. Explain to groups that each student in their group will illustrate one page of their illustrated guide. Clarify that each page will contain one entry and one illustration.

4. Direct groups to think of ways to illustrate the four points of their assigned religions. For example, *kama*, the second goal under Hinduism, might be illustrated by showing a person looking at a beautiful vase.

5. Allow students to illustrate their books using paper and colored pencils or markers. Students may wish to bind their books using a hole punch and colored yarn.

6. After groups have completed their books, allow them to present them to the class. Encourage groups to explain how their drawings illustrate the Buddhist or Hindu concepts.

7. Finally, lead the class in a discussion that compares and contrasts the concepts of Buddhism and Hinduism.

EXTENSION

Groups can conduct further research about Buddhism and Hinduism, using reference books or the Internet. Allow students to discuss their findings and share them with the class.

A Guide to Buddhism and Hinduism

Two ancient religions of India are Buddhism and Hinduism. Below are some of the teachings for these religions. Work with others to create a book about Buddhism or Hinduism. Illustrate each teaching on a separate page in your book.

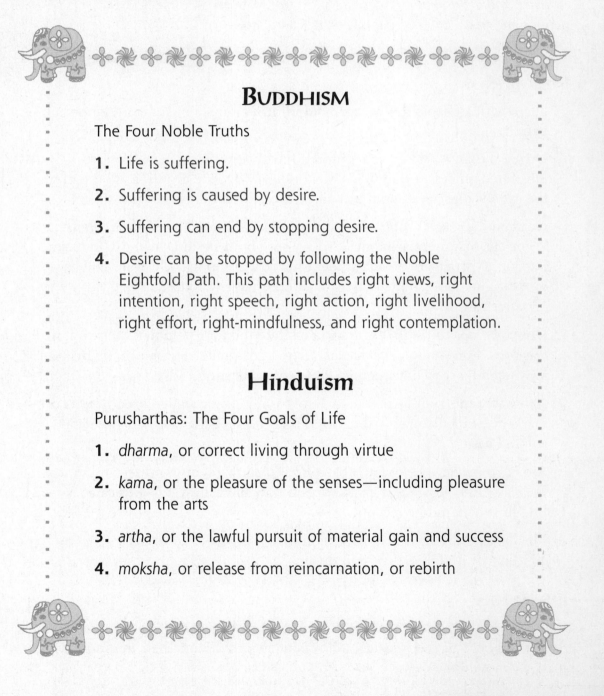

Buddhism

The Four Noble Truths

1. Life is suffering.

2. Suffering is caused by desire.

3. Suffering can end by stopping desire.

4. Desire can be stopped by following the Noble Eightfold Path. This path includes right views, right intention, right speech, right action, right livelihood, right effort, right-mindfulness, and right contemplation.

Hinduism

Purusharthas: The Four Goals of Life

1. *dharma*, or correct living through virtue

2. *kama*, or the pleasure of the senses—including pleasure from the arts

3. *artha*, or the lawful pursuit of material gain and success

4. *moksha*, or release from reincarnation, or rebirth

AFRICA

Map and Time Line

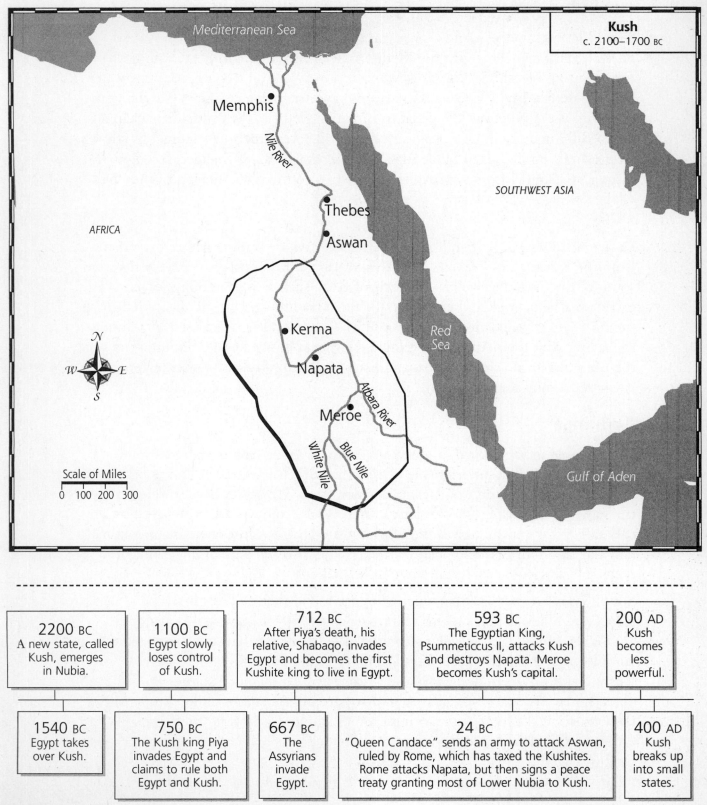

Kush
c. 2100–1700 BC

Mediterranean Sea

SOUTHWEST ASIA

AFRICA

Memphis

Nile River

Thebes

Aswan

Kerma

Napata

Red Sea

Atbara River

Meroe

White Nile

Blue Nile

Gulf of Aden

N
W E
S

Scale of Miles
0 100 200 300

2200 BC
A new state, called Kush, emerges in Nubia.

1540 BC
Egypt takes over Kush.

1100 BC
Egypt slowly loses control of Kush.

750 BC
The Kush king Piya invades Egypt and claims to rule both Egypt and Kush.

712 BC
After Piya's death, his relative, Shabaqo, invades Egypt and becomes the first Kushite king to live in Egypt.

667 BC
The Assyrians invade Egypt.

593 BC
The Egyptian King, Psummeticcus II, attacks Kush and destroys Napata. Meroe becomes Kush's capital.

24 BC
"Queen Candace" sends an army to attack Aswan, ruled by Rome, which has taxed the Kushites. Rome attacks Napata, but then signs a peace treaty granting most of Lower Nubia to Kush.

200 AD
Kush becomes less powerful.

400 AD
Kush breaks up into small states.

49

Geography and Architecture

The Nile River

The Nile River is the world's longest river at 4,145 miles (6,671 km). It flows north from the equator into the Mediterranean Sea. It was important to both Egyptians and Kushites. Kushites, who lived in a very dry region, used the water of the Nile for drinking, cleaning, bathing, and irrigating crops. While the yearly flooding of the Nile was beneficial to Egyptian farmers, the Nile's deep channels in Kush limited flooding. Locations on the Nile are sometimes defined by the river's cataracts (rapids or falls). Although the size of Kush changed throughout its history, it spanned from approximately the first to the sixth cataract of the Nile.

Trade

Kush traded with Egypt and other civilizations. Many trading routes extended from the Kushite city of Meroe (MARE-o-way). Through Kush came items from south of the Sahara as well as products of Kush such as ivory, ebony, leopard skins, ostrich feathers, gold, and emeralds. To reach trading centers, people sailed along the Nile and traveled along caravan routes, which cut across deserts. In addition to trading with their African neighbors, Kush was connected by trading routes to the Mediterranean, the Red Sea, and Asia—especially India. As a center of trade, Kush's economy thrived.

Buildings

Most people in Kush lived in rectangular homes made from sun-baked mud, while others lived in homes made of palm wood. These wooden homes had flat roofs with beams made from acadia or palm trees. Wealthier homes were built in the same fashion using fire-hardened brick. These homes had a courtyard on the east side to take advantage of the morning sunlight. Kushites who herded animals may have lived in portable beehive-shaped huts covered with animal skins or reeds. Herds-people sometimes put an ostrich egg on top of their huts for luck.

Some Kushite cities were surrounded by walls and moats. They included streets, palaces, temples, government buildings, shrines with fountains, observatories, and baths. Homes and temples also existed outside the city walls. Large temple complexes, some with panels of gold that reflected the sun, paid homage to Kushite and Egyptian deities. These temples, which included statues and other objects, may also have served as schools where priests taught children of wealthy families. Rich Kushites built pyramid tombs similar to those of the Egyptians. Other buildings included those for manufacturing, which contained furnaces for smelting iron.

READING MAPS OF THE NILE RIVER

Students use maps to answer questions about the Nile River.

MATERIALS

globes, maps of northern Africa, *A Map of the Nile* (page 52), pencils or pens, paper

HERE'S HOW

1 Use maps and globes to point out to students where Egypt and Kush were located. Point out that Kush occupied territory in what is now part of northern Sudan. Ask students to list geographical features on the maps and globes that they see in northern Sudan. *(Students may list such features as the Nubian Desert, Bayuda Desert, Red Sea, and Nile River.)*

2 Ask students to tell you what they notice about the areas surrounding the Nile River. *(There are cities there.)* Ask students why cities would be around the Nile River. Make a list of their ideas on the board. Share with students the background information about the Nile River on page 50.

3 Have students imagine that the drinking fountains at their school are their only source of water. Have students work in groups of three or four to create a list on a piece of paper of the ways this would change their lives.

4 Let each group share their list with the class.

5 Have students imagine that they live in ancient Kush along the Nile River. Then have them write a short story about how their family copes with getting water.

6 Give students copies of *A Map of the Nile*. Point out the map of ancient Kush. Explain that the cataracts of the Nile River are rapids or falls.

7 In a location that students can easily access, place a map of modern Africa that includes cities along the Nile River. Have students compare their map on *A Map of the Nile* with the modern map. Ask students to find things on their maps that still exist today. Make a list on the board. *(Answers will vary according to the modern map used. Possible answers: Memphis [Cairo], Aswan, Macoraba [Mecca], Adane [Aden], Aksum, Jerusalem, Red Sea, Nile River, White Nile, Blue Nile, Atbara River, Mediterranean Sea, Lybian Desert, Arabian Desert)* Then ask students to find things on their maps that no longer exist. Make another list on the board. *(Possible answers: Thebes, Napata, Soba, Berenice, Coptos, Adulis, Meroe)*

8 Have students use the map on *A Map of the Nile* to answer the questions at the bottom of the page.

Answers
1. Memphis 2. six 3. Meroe is located within a triangle of rivers. 4. the Red Sea. 5. Soba

A Map of the Nile

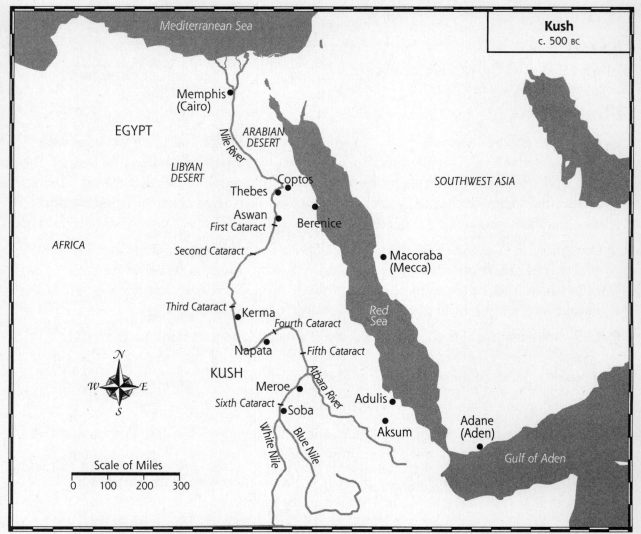

Use the map to answer the following questions.

1. If you enter the Nile River at the delta, what big city will you come to first?

_____

2. How many cataracts are there on the Nile River? _____

3. Why might people say that the city of Meroe was located within a triangle? _____

_____

4. What large body of water lies east of Kush? _____

5. At which Kushite city does the Nile River split into the Blue Nile and White Nile?

_____

Ancient Civilizations: China, India, Africa, Mesopotamia Scholastic Teaching Resources

A Game of Kushite Trade

Students play a game about trade in ancient Kush.

MATERIALS

a transparency of the map on *A Map of the Nile* (page 52), overhead projector, colored overhead markers, *Kushite Trade Game Board* (page 54), *Trading Cards* (page 55), scissors, dice (one per group), one game marker per student (such as a dried bean or a penny)

HERE'S HOW

❶ Create a transparency of the map on *A Map of the Nile*.

❷ Explain to students that Kushite society depended on its relations with foreign trade partners. Show students the transparency of the map of ancient Kush. Ask students with whom they think the Kushites might have traded. Write students' suggestions on the board or on the transparency.

❸ Share with students the background information about Kushite trade on page 50. Using different colored overhead markers to represent different routes, show students a rough idea of some trading routes by drawing the following: a line along land from Memphis to Macoraba to Adane; a line through the Red Sea from Adane to Adulis; a line along land from Adulis to Meroe; and a line through the desert from Meroe to Napata, then along the Nile to the Mediterranean Sea.

❹ Tell students that they will be playing a game based on Kushite trade. Divide the class into groups of three to five students.

❺ Distribute a die and one copy of the *Kushite Trade Game Board* to each group. Give each student a game marker and a copy of *Trading Cards*.

❻ Have students cut out their 12 trading cards. Explain to students that the game cards represent items that Kushites traded. Tell students that the goal of the game is to have a successful trading expedition by meeting their trading goal.

❼ For each round of play, have players agree on a trading goal such as: *to be the first trader to finish the game with eight cards, four of ivory and four of gold* or, for a longer game, *to be the first trader to finish the game with five cards, all of the same type of good.*

❽ Have each player roll the die. The player who rolls the highest number goes first.

❾ Explain these rules to students:
- To begin, players place their markers on the city of Meroe.
- Players roll the die and move their markers the corresponding number of spaces.
- Players can move in any direction.
- Players must follow the directions on the spaces.
- The first player to achieve his or her trading goal wins.

Kushite Trade Game Board

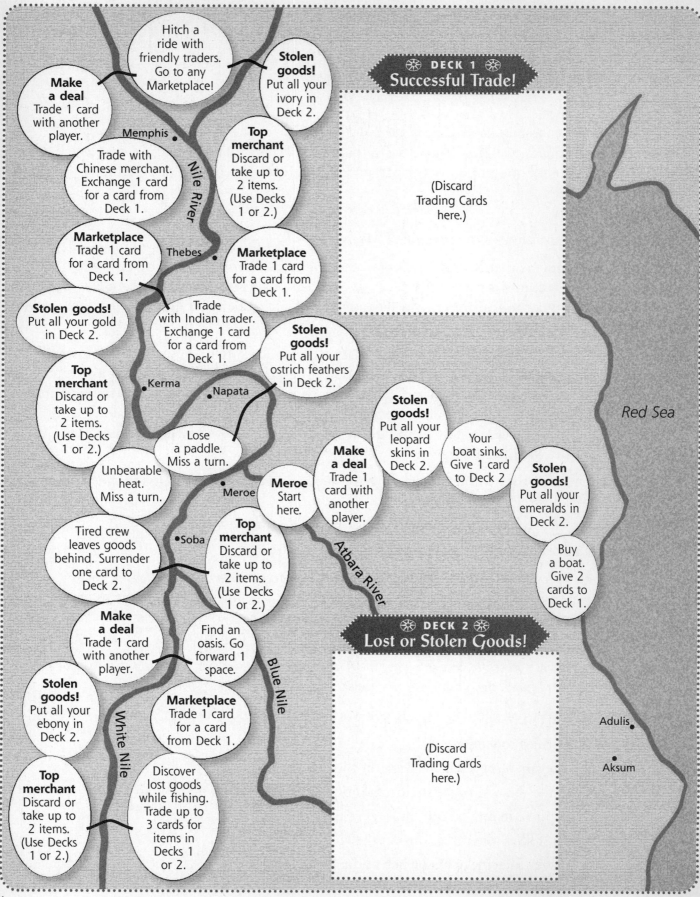

Hitch a ride with friendly traders. Go to any Marketplace!

Make a deal
Trade 1 card with another player.

Memphis

Trade with Chinese merchant. Exchange 1 card for a card from Deck 1.

Nile River

Stolen goods!
Put all your ivory in Deck 2.

Top merchant
Discard or take up to 2 items. (Use Decks 1 or 2.)

Marketplace
Trade 1 card for a card from Deck 1.

Thebes

Marketplace
Trade 1 card for a card from Deck 1.

Stolen goods!
Put all your gold in Deck 2.

Trade with Indian trader. Exchange 1 card for a card from Deck 1.

Stolen goods!
Put all your ostrich feathers in Deck 2.

**⊛ DECK 1 ⊛
Successful Trade!**

(Discard Trading Cards here.)

Top merchant
Discard or take up to 2 items. (Use Decks 1 or 2.)

Kerma

Napata

Lose a paddle. Miss a turn.

Unbearable heat. Miss a turn.

Meroe

Stolen goods!
Put all your leopard skins in Deck 2.

Your boat sinks. Give 1 card to Deck 2

Stolen goods!
Put all your emeralds in Deck 2.

Red Sea

Make a deal
Trade 1 card with another player.

Meroe
Start here.

Atbara River

Buy a boat. Give 2 cards to Deck 1.

Tired crew leaves goods behind. Surrender one card to Deck 2.

Soba

Top merchant
Discard or take up to 2 items. (Use Decks 1 or 2.)

Find an oasis. Go forward 1 space.

**⊛ DECK 2 ⊛
Lost or Stolen Goods!**

Make a deal
Trade 1 card with another player.

Blue Nile

Stolen goods!
Put all your ebony in Deck 2.

Marketplace
Trade 1 card for a card from Deck 1.

White Nile

(Discard Trading Cards here.)

Adulis

Top merchant
Discard or take up to 2 items. (Use Decks 1 or 2.)

Discover lost goods while fishing. Trade up to 3 cards for items in Decks 1 or 2.

Aksum

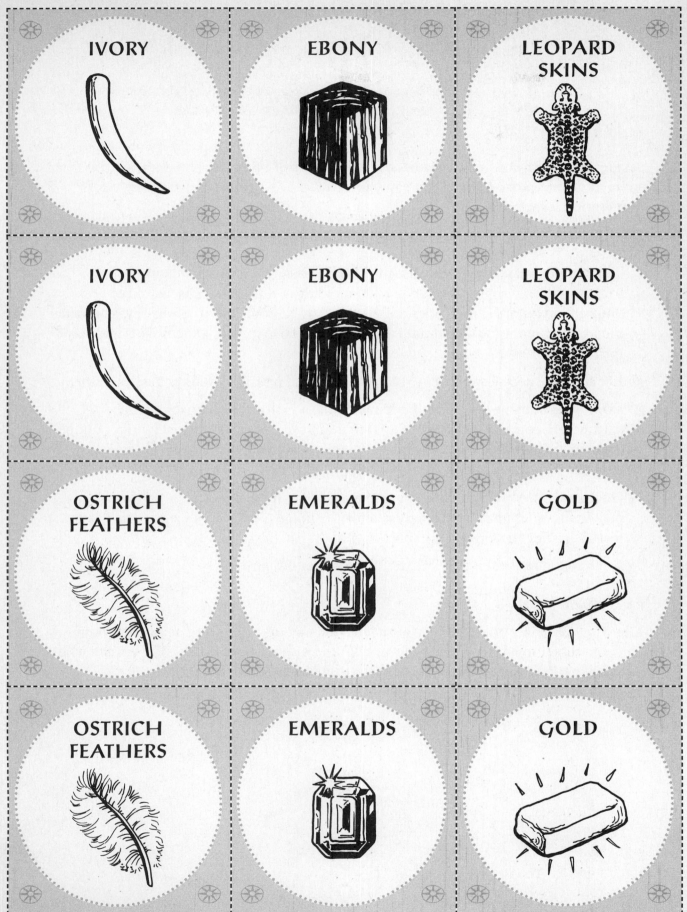

Building a Home in Kush

Students design, sketch, and build a Kushite home.

Materials

paper; pencils; various building materials such as small boxes, cardboard, plastic milk containers, juice boxes, aluminum cans, and plastic bags; glue; tape; scissors; snacks brought in by students

Here's How

1. This activity may take place over a few days. First, share with students the background information about Kushite buildings on page 50. Discuss three different styles of Kushite homes: fire-baked brick homes for the wealthy, sun-baked mud brick homes for the common class, and beehive huts of animal skins and reeds for nomads.

2. Let students decide which style of home to build, or assign different styles to them.

3. Work with students to collect building supplies such as small boxes, cardboard, plastic milk containers, juice boxes, aluminum cans, or other items. Supplies can be collected from other classrooms, the cafeteria, and students' homes. On building day, divvy up the supplies.

4. Have students sketch preliminary drawings of the homes they plan to build. You may wish to designate a standard size for the homes—such as a length of at least five inches for the base of the shortest wall.

5. After you approve the sketches, let students build their homes.

Extension

After the homes are complete, have students plan an open house to show their homes. Students should plan what they want to tell others about their home. Allow students to bring in snacks for others to enjoy as they "visit" each other's homes.

Arts and Sciences

The Game of Wari

Some archaeologists believe the Kushite people may have played the ancient game of Wari. This game, which is a type of Mancala game, is thought to have originated in Egypt thousands of years ago. The Wari game board is made from wood or hardened clay; sometimes the game is played on the ground. Game boards include six holes on each side. Players use pebbles, seeds, or other small objects as game pieces. The object of the game is to capture the most game pieces. Today, Wari is still played in Africa and other parts of the world.

The Meroitic Language

Much about the people of Kush remains a mystery because their writing cannot be understood. During the early days, Kushites used Egyptian hieroglyphs. After the capital of Kush moved to Meroe, Kushites developed their own hieroglyphics and cursive writing called Meroitic. Although scholars believe that Kushites spoke Meiotic as long ago as 750 BC, the language was probably not written down until 300 years later. Using an alphabet of 23 letters, the language was written in one direction with dots separating the words. Inscriptions of names have been found written in both Meroitic and Egyptian, allowing scholars to assign sounds to specific letters. When archaeologists find tablets written in both Meroitic and another known language, such as Egyptian or Greek, they may be better able to understand this mysterious language.

Ironworkers

When the Assyrians conquered Kushite Egypt in 671 BC, they had iron weapons, which were far superior to the copper and bronze weapons in Egypt and Kush. Although the conquerors may have wanted to keep the process of iron making a secret to maintain their military superiority, Kushites discovered the secrets of producing iron. Meroe had natural resources necessary for making iron and became the major iron center of Africa. Among Meroe's natural resources were iron ore and charcoal fuel, which was gathered from the forests of acacia trees near the Nile. To manufacture iron, the nonmetallic and metallic parts of the ore were separated in a process called *smelting*. Iron ore, charcoal, and lime were placed in clay furnaces. After heating these ingredients for hours, iron emerged that could be made into tools or weapons.

WARI: AN AFRICAN GAME

Students play a version of the African game Wari.

MATERIALS

egg cartons (one for each pair of students); 48 pebbles, marbles, or other small objects to be used as game markers (for each pair of students); paper; pencils or pens

HERE'S HOW

1 Divide the class into pairs. Give each pair an egg carton and 48 pebbles or markers. Share with students the background information about Wari on page 57.

2 Have players each choose one side of the board and place four markers in each of their six holes. Explain that the object of the game is to capture more markers than your opponent. Relay the following rules to pairs:

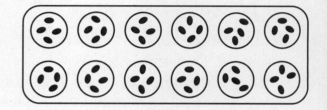

- Players alternate turns.

- Players always begin their turn on their own side of the board.

- Markers always move counter-clockwise around the board.

- The first player takes all four markers from any hole on his or her side and drops them, one at a time, into the following four holes.

- If the last marker lands in an opponent's hole with two or three markers, the player captures those markers and removes them from the board. If the opponent's holes next to that hole also have two or three markers, the player captures those as well.

- Markers are distributed in the same way, no matter how many markers are in one hole. For example, a hole with seven markers is distributed to the next seven holes.

- If a hole has twelve or more markers, a player drops them into succeeding holes, but skips over the hole from which they originated.

- When a player's holes are all empty and unable to be filled by an opponent, the player wins the remaining markers left on the board.

EXTENSION

Have students use only pebbles or small markers to create a game for the people of Kush. Have students write the rules for their games. Then let students share their games with the class.

Writing the Language of Kush

Students write Meroitic in both hieroglyphics and cursive script.

Materials

Meroitic Writing (page 60), dictionary, paper, pencils or pens

Here's How

1. Distribute copies of *Meroitic Writing* to students.

2. Ask students to examine the Meroitic language. Direct them to compare the hieroglyphics and cursive scripts. Allow students to comment on any similarities that they see.

3. Share with students the background information about the Meroitic language on page 57. Emphasize the difference between understanding how sounds in a word are pronounced and knowing what the word means. For an example, use a dictionary to look up an unfamiliar word. Use the pronunciation key to say the word. Emphasize that knowing how to pronounce a word is different from knowing the word's meaning.

4. Tell students that they will be using the Meroitic script to write words. Have students follow the directions on *Meroitic Writing*.

5. Have students trade papers and try to decipher one another's words.

Extension

Let students create their own language. Have them tell about the history of their language, who used it, and what it looks like. Students should submit a sample "alphabet" or sign list for their language.

MEROITIC WRITING

Use the chart below to write your own Meroitic words on a separate sheet of paper. Write some words in hieroglyphics and others in cursive script.

Hieroglyph	Cursive	Phonetic Value	Hieroglyph	Cursive	Phonetic Value
		a			l
		e			kh
		i			kh
		o			sh
		y			s (se)
		w			k
		b			q
		p			t
		m			te
		n			to
		ne			d
		r			word divider

Ancient Civilizations: China, India, Africa, Mesopotamia   Scholastic Teaching Resources

How to Make Iron

Students write a story about uncovering the secret of iron making.

MATERIALS

paper, pencils or pens, reference books or the Internet

HERE'S HOW

❶ Ask students to identify objects in their society (or in the classroom) that are made from iron.

❷ Share with students the background information about Kushite ironworkers on page 57. Discuss with students why the Assyrians might have wanted to keep the secret of iron making to themselves. Help students to realize that once Kush was able to produce its own iron weapons, it was better able to defend itself.

❸ Present students with the following scenario: "You live in ancient Kush. The Assyrians have conquered your people with iron weapons. You need to find out the secret of making these weapons. You sneak into an iron-making workshop disguised as an Assyrian worker and discover how it is done." Ask students to use reference sources on early iron-making, such as Ruth G. Kassinger's *Iron and Steel*, to write a short how-to paragraph that lists the materials needed and the basic steps. Encourage them to leave a wide margin to illustrate the materials or the process.

❹ Let students compare their paragraphs with a partner and revise based on the partner's feedback. Partners should check that the writer included the following: all necessary materials and tools, all steps in order, and introductory and concluding sentences.

EXTENSION

Have students create a list of iron items that they would make for Kush society. *(Students might list spear points, axes, hoes, and other weapons or tools.)*

GOVERNMENT AND RELIGION

Queen Candace

Upon the death of Kushite kings, queens could rule until their sons were old enough to take the throne. Later in Kush history, Kushite queens often ruled alone or with their husbands or sons. Candace (KAN-DA-key) is a Kushite title derived from the ancient Kushite word for *queen* or *queen mother*. Other countries sometimes confused this title with the queen's name. In 24 BC the Romans gained control of Egypt and tried to tax the people of northern Kush. Angry at the taxation of her people, "Queen Candace"—thought to be a Kushite queen called Amanirenas—ordered the Kushite army to attack what is now Aswan, Egypt. There the Kushites cut off the head of a statue of the Roman emperor Augustus. They took the head to Meroe and buried it symbolically under the doorway of an important building. In retaliation, the Romans attacked Napata, the former capital of Kush. Soon after, a peace treaty was negotiated between the Romans and the Kushites. Some scholars believe that the Romans respected the Kushite's military strength. The peace treaty resulted in the return of Kush's conquered lands and the removal of the tax.

Kushite Rulers

The best-known Kushite rulers are those from the 25th dynasty in Egypt. Around 750 BC a Kushite king name Piankhy—also called Piya or Piye—invaded Egypt. In 726 BC he attacked Egypt again, expanding his rule. After Piankhy died, his relative Shabaqo ruled Egypt and Kush, becoming the first Kushite king to live in Egypt. Shabaqo accepted many Egyptian traditions and established diplomatic relations with foreign kings. After the reign of Shabaqo, Shebitqo, took the throne. He faced threats from the Assyrian kings, in what is now Iraq. Shebitqo created military alliances with other nations to defeat the Assyrians. His brother, Taharqa, aided him in the fight and became king after Shebitqo's death. Although he had a successful reign at first, his army succumbed to the Assyrians, who persisted in attacking Egypt. Kushite rulers continued to rule from Kush. One ruler, Arnekhamani, built a huge temple to the lion god Apedemak.

Kushite Gods

Because of their contact with Egypt, Kushites worshipped a combination of Egyptian and Kushite deities. Although Kushites worshipped many gods, they believed that the gods were different forms of the god Amun. Both Egyptian and Kushite kings traveled to worship Amun near Napata, where the deity was thought to dwell inside a small mountain. Some scholars believe there may have been at least fifteen temples in front of this holy mountain, known today as Jewel Baikal. Believed to be various manifestations of Amun, Kushite gods often changed forms and names. One native Kushite god was the lion-headed warrior god Apedemak, who is thought to have protected the Kushite kings. Artwork and sculptures of lions appeared throughout the Kushite kingdom. In many drawings Apedemak has the body of a man or a snake.

A Kushite Conflict Reenactment

Students reenact a conflict between Kushites and Romans and create a peace treaty.

MATERIALS

masking tape, *Queen Candace Cards* (pages 64–65), scissors, small, individually wrapped pieces of hard candy (pennies, marbles, or other small objects are fine substitutions), paper, pencils or pens

HERE'S HOW

1. Before students come to class, divide the room in half using masking tape. Copy and cut out *Queen Candace Cards*. If needed, copy and cut out additional cards for Northern and Southern Kushites, so that all students will receive cards.

2. As each student enters the room, give him or her a piece of wrapped candy. Tell students not to eat it or unwrap it. In addition, give each student a card.

3. Tell students that they will reenact a Kushite conflict with the Romans. Share with students the background information about Queen Candace on page 62. Explain to students that their cards reveal their identities and what they should do in the reenactment.

4. Tell students that the north, controlled by the Romans, is where the teacher's desk (or another classroom landmark) is located. Explain that the Roman emperor will sit at this spot. Point out that the other side of the room represents the south, which is controlled by the Kushite queen.

5. Let students act out the information on their cards. Direct students to react to the events going on around them, even if they do not have speaking parts.

6. When students finish acting out the scene, ask them what they think the treaty between the Kushites and the Romans might have said: What might each side have agreed to do to be a better neighbor to the other? (You may need to explain a treaty as a written peace agreement in which each side promises to take certain actions that will benefit the other side.)

7. Have students work in groups of three to four to write a treaty.

8. Post the treaties for everyone to read.

The Roman Emperor

You are the Roman emperor. Your throne is the teacher's desk. Quickly take a sheet of paper and draw a full-body statue of yourself. Place it on the desk. You will be the first to talk. Say: "I am the Roman emperor, Augustus! Behold the statue of me! I rule Egypt and all the surrounding areas, including the Kushites! I demand that everyone in the north pay me a tax!" Make sure that everyone on your side of the line gives you their candy.

SPEAKER 1

Kushite Messenger

You are a messenger living on the north side of the country. After the northern Kushites pay the Roman emperor their taxes (candy), sneak out and go over the line to the queen of Kush. Say: "Mighty queen! The Roman emperor is taxing your people in the northern part of Kush!"

SPEAKER 2

Kushite Prince

You are the prince of Kush. After the people applaud the queen's speech, say: "We will take the statue of the Roman emperor and cut off its head!" Go with your mother, the queen, to attack the Romans in northern Kush. While you are there, take the picture of the emperor and tear off the head. Take the picture of the head back to southern Kush, and bury it under a desk.

SPEAKER 4

The Kushite Queen

You are the Kushite queen. You live in the south part of Kush. When the messenger comes to you with news of the Roman tax, say: "How dare the Roman emperor think he can tax us, the mighty Kush nation! We will not pay the tax! In fact, we will teach him a lesson by attacking Roman forts." Your people applaud your speech. Wait for your son, the prince, to talk. Then take your son, along with the army, to the Roman emperor's throne (the teacher's desk). With your guard, take all the tax (candy) from the throne. Then give it back to your people living in the north.

SPEAKER 3

Kushite Guard

You are a guard in southern Kush. When you hear the queen tell of her anger about the tax, join the queen and go into northern Kush. Assist the queen in taking the tax (candy) from the emperor's throne (teacher's desk). Then give it back to the people in the north. Follow your queen and prince back home. Watch as the prince buries a picture of the emperor's head under a desk. Then say: "Yes, burying this head of the statue of the Roman emperor Augustus is a great way to show him that he is under your feet. The doorway is a wonderful place for this!"

SPEAKER 5

Southern Kushite

You live in southern Kush. You are under the direct rule of your queen. Applaud the queen after she says her lines. Then applaud the prince after he says his lines.

Northern Kushite

You live in northern Kush. When the Roman emperor demands a tax, give the emperor your candy.

Southern Kushite

You live in southern Kush. You are under the direct rule of your queen. Applaud the queen after she says her lines. Then applaud the prince after he says his lines.

Northern Kushite

You live in northern Kush. When the Roman emperor demands a tax, give the emperor your candy.

Southern Kushite

You live in southern Kush. You are under the direct rule of your queen. Applaud the queen after she says her lines. Then applaud the prince after he says his lines.

Northern Kushite

You live in northern Kush. When the Roman emperor demands a tax, give the emperor your candy.

THE KUSHITE DYNASTY DINNER PARTY

Students create a seating plan for a royal Kushite dinner party.

MATERIALS

A Seating Plan (page 67), pencils or pens

HERE'S HOW

❶ Share with students the background information about Kushite rulers on page 62.

❷ Tell students that they will plan a dinner party for some of Kush's most celebrated rulers. Explain that some of these rulers lived during different time periods.

❸ Distribute copies of *A Seating Plan* to students. Let students work individually or in small groups to complete the activity.

Answer

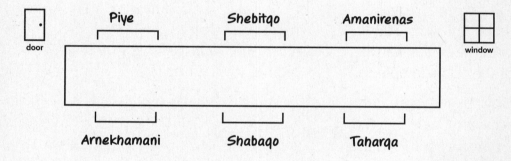

A Seating Plan

You are in charge of arranging a dinner for some of the Kushite rulers. They all have particular ideas about whom they want to sit near. You must carefully plan the seating. These rulers will be seated at a rectangular table with three rulers on each side. No one will sit at the heads of the table. Use the clues below to accomplish your job.

Piye: King Piye, who was the first Kush king to take control of a large part of Egypt, ruled from about 747 BC to 716 BC. Piye, a horse lover, was buried near the graves of four of his horses. He wants to sit nearest to the door. He also wants to sit across from the one responsible for making Apedemak, the lion god, popular.

Shabaqo: As the first Kushite king to make Egypt his home, Shabaqo made the Egyptian city of Memphis the capital. Sometimes called the founder of the 25th Dynasty of Egypt, Shabaqo ruled from about 716 BC to 702 BC. Shabaqo wants to sit in between the warrior king and the builder of the "Lion Temple."

Shebitqo: When the Assyrians attacked the land along the Mediterranean Sea, Shebitqo joined with Israeli kings to stop the Assyrians, who abandoned the takeover because of illness. Shebitqo, who ruled from about 702 BC to 690 BC, wants to sit next to the queen who drove back the Romans and discuss battle tactics.

Taharqa: Known as a warrior king, Taharqa led Shebitqo's army when he was 20 years old. He ruled from about 690 BC to 664 BC. During his early years, the Nile flooded and caused large harvests, profiting his kingdom. Taharqa demands to sit across from the only queen attending.

Arnekhamani: This king, who ruled from about 235 to 218 BC, was famous for building the "Lion Temple" and encouraging the worship of Apedemak. He supported the development of art and architecture. In addition to discussing his love of lions, Arnekhamani wants to talk about horses and sit across from the horse lover.

Amanirenas: Called Candace by the Romans, this queen ruled from about 40 BC to 10 BC. She attacked the Romans in what is now Aswan in Egypt and then brokered a peace treaty with them. She was also blind in one eye. She wants to sit at the end of the table near the window.

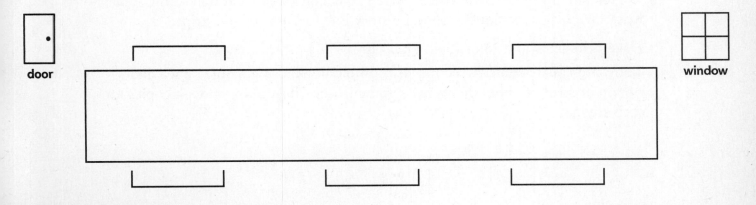

door   window

A Comic Strip of the Lion King

Students create a comic strip featuring the Kushite god Apedemek.

Materials

paper, colored pencils, hole punch, ribbon or string

Here's How

❶ Write the following on the chalkboard:
Hymn of Apedemek:
"Lion of the South, strong of arm, great god . . . who will not be hindered in heaven and earth, who provides nourishment for all men, who hurls his hot breath against the enemy, the one who punishes all who commit crimes against him, who prepares a place for those who give themselves to him, who gives to those who call to him, Lord of life."

❷ Ask students if they know the names of any ancient gods. Some students might be familiar with Egyptian gods such as Osiris, Isis, or Horus; Greek gods such as Zeus, Apollo, or Athena; and Roman gods such as Neptune, Jupiter, or Mars. On the board, list these gods.

❸ Ask students to think about possible reasons that these civilizations worshipped a variety of gods. List these ideas on the board. *(Possible answers: people prayed to the gods for good harvests, good weather, to win battles, and so on.)*

❹ Ask students to identify the purposes of each god. List the purposes on the board. *(Possible examples: Poseidon was god of the sea, earthquakes, and horses; and so on.)*

❺ Tell students that Kushites also worshipped gods. Share the background information about Kushite gods on page 62. Then read the hymn of Apedemek that you wrote on the board.

❻ Group students in pairs. Tell pairs that they will create a comic strip about Apedemek.

❼ Direct pairs to think about the Hymn of Apedemek and what they know about Kush civilization as they sketch out a story line for their comic strips.

❽ Have pairs draw and color their comic strips on a piece of paper.

❾ Copy and collate students' comic strips into a book, using a hole punch and ribbon or string to bind the pages together. If possible, make enough copies for each student.

SOLVING A MYSTERY OF THE GODS

Students solve a mystery involving Kushite gods.

MATERIALS

Interview Clues (pages 71–72), *A Weather Mystery* (page 70), scissors, envelopes, paper, pencils or pens

HERE'S HOW

1️⃣ Copy and cut out *Interview Clues*. Place each clue in a separate envelope. Label each envelope with the corresponding deity's name on the interview clue.

2️⃣ Distribute *A Weather Mystery* to students and read aloud "The Mystery." Tell students that they will act as detectives to uncover the identities of Kushite gods and goddesses in order to reveal which deities are responsible for the weather.

3️⃣ Place the envelopes in a location that students can easily access. Explain to students that each envelope contains clues about the deities of Kush, including their alibis. Direct students to take turns requesting the envelopes.

4️⃣ Ask students to consult the information on *A Weather Mystery* to help them solve the case. Direct students to put check marks near the names of the suspects that they believe are involved in the mystery. Tell students who have solved the case to keep the information confidential until everyone in the class has solved the mystery.

5️⃣ When all students have recorded their answers, tell students that the culprits are Sekhmet, Tefnut, and Shu. Read the following myth to the class. Explain that this is one version that tells how Kushites explained the seasons and weather.

An angry Sekhmet ran away from home after her father, Atum, finished creating the universe. Her angry, flaming breath burned the fields during summer. The hard rains of Tefnut followed Sekhmet's burning heat. In the fall, Shu sent cooling winds from the north to vanish the heat and rain. In this way, Shu calmed his sisters.

A WEATHER MYSTERY

It is your job to solve a mystery for the Kushite people! Read the information below. Then, examine the files on Kush's gods and goddesses. Use the process of deduction to uncover the culprits. Put a check mark next to the suspects that you think are guilty.

The Mystery

Harsh and unpredictable weather has been plaguing the land of Kush for many years. The Kushites awoke this morning to steady winds from the north. After the past few months of suffering under the midsummer's terrible heat and then violent rains, most people were relieved to have the cooling winds. Many Kushites want to get to the bottom of this weather trend. Who is responsible for this weather? Can it be stopped? You've been hired by the Kushites to solve this mystery!

What We Know

❋ This weather trend happens every year from summer through fall.

❋ The job is too big for just one god or goddess. More than one deity has to be involved.

❋ Many people have reported seeing lion-headed creatures in the area.

❋ During the midsummer months, the land looks as if it has been burned by fire.

List of Suspects

☐ Apedemak   ☐ Khnum

☐ Atum   ☐ Sekhmet

☐ Bes   ☐ Shu

☐ Hapi   ☐ Tefnut

Ancient Civilizations: China, India, Africa, Mesopotamia Scholastic Teaching Resources

APEDEMAK

Throughout the year, the lion-headed god Apedemak says that he stays busy protecting the Kushite king. He claims to have little time for anything else.

ATUM

This sun god sometimes has the head of a ram. He says he came about by rising from a swamp. From that point on, he began creating. This includes Earth, the gods, the heavens, and more. He is the father of the twin gods Shu and Tefnut. He admits that his daughter, Sekhmet, is uncontrollable and has asked his son, Shu, to do something about it.

BES

This friendly god has short legs and is part lion. He spends much of his time dancing, singing, and drinking. When asked about Sekhmet, he says that he spends time with her, trying to keep her calm and happy with his jokes. He says he also protects people from snakes and scorpions.

HAPI

Hapi, who is rather plump, is in charge of the Nile River all year long. He claims that he never leaves the river, and is always busy bringing gifts to the river. He insists he has nothing to do with the violent rains. He says that Khnum is almost always by the first cataract of the Nile.

KHNUM

This god, who has the head of a ram, spends all his time at the Nile's cataracts (areas with rapids). He admits that he is responsible for making the river flood, but denies that he has anything to do with the heavy rains that have been occurring. Khnum verifies that Hapi was by the Nile.

SEKHMET

This lion-headed goddess has a hard time getting along with her father, Atum. In fact, just after he created the world she ran away. She has a long criminal record of assaulting humans and burning fields with her fiery breath. She says she sometimes visits with Bes, who tries to make her laugh and keep her in a good mood. Her brother Shu also tries to control her temper.

SHU

Shu, the god of life, air, and wind, looks like a man. Sometimes people show him as a lion along with his twin sister, Tefnut. Shu's father, Atum, has been begging him to find his runaway sister, Sekmet, and return her to him. Although Shu is a very popular god with the Kushites, he seems uncooperative during the investigation.

TEFNUT

This lion-headed goddess is often confused with Sekhmet. She denies claims that she burns the land with her breath. As the goddess of moisture and rain, she wonders if her lot was cast by her father, Atum—who created her and her twin brother, Shu, out of his spit. Tefnut refuses to further describe her relationships with Shu and Sekhmet.

Mesopotamia
Map and Time Line

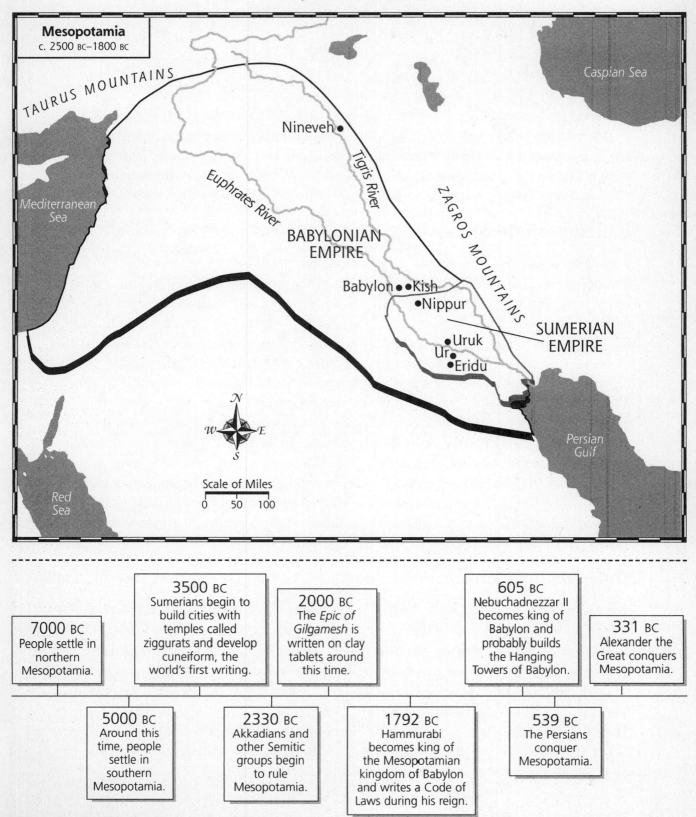

Mesopotamia
c. 2500 BC–1800 BC

TAURUS MOUNTAINS

Caspian Sea

Mediterranean Sea

Nineveh

Tigris River

Euphrates River

ZAGROS MOUNTAINS

BABYLONIAN EMPIRE

Babylon • • Kish
• Nippur

SUMERIAN EMPIRE

• Uruk
Ur •
• Eridu

N
W E
S

Persian Gulf

Scale of Miles
0   50   100

Red Sea

7000 BC
People settle in northern Mesopotamia.

5000 BC
Around this time, people settle in southern Mesopotamia.

3500 BC
Sumerians begin to build cities with temples called ziggurats and develop cuneiform, the world's first writing.

2330 BC
Akkadians and other Semitic groups begin to rule Mesopotamia.

2000 BC
The *Epic of Gilgamesh* is written on clay tablets around this time.

1792 BC
Hammurabi becomes king of the Mesopotamian kingdom of Babylon and writes a Code of Laws during his reign.

605 BC
Nebuchadnezzar II becomes king of Babylon and probably builds the Hanging Towers of Babylon.

539 BC
The Persians conquer Mesopotamia.

331 BC
Alexander the Great conquers Mesopotamia.

Geography and Architecture

Land and Water

Mesopotamia means the land between the rivers. It was situated on the land surrounding the Tigris and Euphrates Rivers in what is primarily modern Iraq. Because these two rivers flooded, Mesopotamians created water control systems and used irrigation to bring water to their crops. City-states soon grew along the rivers, forming the great civilization of Mesopotamia. One city-state, Babylon, was located on the Euphrates and became an important trading center. During the 1800s BC, Babylon's king conquered other city-states, creating the Babylonian empire. Some Mesopotamians thought that Babylon was the center of the world.

Building and Decorations

Floods dominated Mesopotamia, causing the land to fill with clay and silt. Mesopotamians used these materials to build their homes and temples. Some walls were decorated with cone mosaics. These small clay cones were placed into walls with the pointed end facing inwards. The flat ends of the mosaics were painted and formed decorative patterns. In addition to looking beautiful, these mosaics helped to protect a building's mud brick walls from deteriorating. Mesopotamian ziggurats, or temples, were made of bricks that were both sun-baked and fired. They were composed of a series of layers that looked like steps, with each layer getting smaller as it rose toward the top. Ziggurats were taller than other buildings and located in the center of cities. Some scholars believe the Tower of Babel, noted in the Bible, is the most well known ziggurat. Mesopotamians created votives, or small statues, to be placed in ziggurats. These intricately carved stone statues vary in design. They have exaggerated features with staring eyes and hands folded as if in prayer. They may also hold a libation cup. The statues were put in ziggurats by worshippers. They were thought to intercede with a deity on behalf of a worshipper.

The Hanging Gardens of Babylon

Historians speculate that King Nebuchadnezzar II built the Hanging Gardens around 600 BC to cheer up his wife, Amyitis. Amyitis came from a green, mountainous region, and the flat, sun-baked land of Mesopotamia depressed her. The king tried to make her happy by building an artificial mountain that included rooftop gardens. The Hanging Gardens were irrigated with water lifted by pumps from the Euphrates River. Full-size trees grew upon the multi-terraced rooftops. Several Greek historians described the Hanging Gardens, and it is known as one of the seven wonders of the ancient world. Although many historians believe the gardens did exist, they are not sure about the precise location.

COMPARING ANCIENT AND MODERN MAPS

Students create a map of the universe and compare it with a Mesopotamian map.

MATERIALS

paper, pencils or pens, Internet access, map of the world

HERE'S HOW

1 Tell students to imagine that they are living in a time before the discovery of other planets and galaxies. Ask students to draw a picture of our universe on a sheet of paper including only Earth, the moon, and the sun. Then have students set their maps aside.

2 Share with students the background information on page 74 about Mesopotamia's land and water.

3 Tell students that Mesopotamians are thought to have been the first people to create and use maps. Explain that one of the earliest maps in existence is a small clay tablet that shows a town plan and that it dates to 6200 BC. Tell students that the first known Mesopotamian map of the world was on a two-sided clay tablet, dating to about 600 BC. Show students this map on the following Web site: **http://www.henry-davis.com/MAPS/Ancient%20Web%20Pages/103.html**. Point out that the map shows Babylon as the center of a round earth, surrounded by water. Explain that places on the map are labeled using a writing called cuneiform.

4 Have students look at a current map of the world. Point out that the Babylonian map was skewed to represent what the Babylonians believed their world looked like.

5 Have students look at the universe maps they created. Ask students whether their maps are skewed as well. Explain that on an accurately drawn map of our universe, the sun, would only be a speck along with other stars and galaxies filling the page. Have students compare the Babylonian map with their map of the universe. *(Possible answer: both maps are skewed, both show incorrect centers.)*

DECORATING WITH CONE MOSAICS

Students design and make clay cone mosaics.

MATERIALS

overhead transparency (optional); overhead projector (optional); paper; colored pencils, crayons, or markers; self-hardening clay in a variety of colors; small square or rectangular baking tins; mud or salt dough

HERE'S HOW

1. Share with students the background information about cone mosaics under "Buildings and Decorations" on page 74. Show students the picture of a cone mosaic on this page. You may wish to create an overhead transparency of the cone mosaic to share with students using an overhead projector.

2. Have students create cone mosaic designs for a Mesopotamian home. Tell students that cone mosaics were often arranged to form geometric patterns, such as triangles, diamonds, straight lines, or zigzag lines. Students can color adjoining circles to represent the mosaic on paper. (Make sure the colors they use match those of the clay you have.)

3. Distribute different colors of self-hardening clay to students, and have them roll about 10 to 12 cone shapes. Direct students to make their cones about two to four inches in length and one inch in diameter at the base. (The length of the cone stem may depend on the depth of the tin students will use and the amount of clay you have available.)

4. To avoid making a mess, have students work outside if possible. After the clay cones have hardened, have pairs or groups of three students gather with their clay cones and the mosaic designs they drew. Tell them they will make a section of a wall mosaic and let them choose one of the designs from their group as their model.

5. Give each group a baking tin filled with mud or dough as deep as the length of the cone stems. Have students arrange the cones in the mud base according to the chosen pattern. Advise them to set the cones point-side down and fit them together closely. When all the cones have been placed, set the tins aside to dry. After the mud has dried, display the mosaic sections with the drawn designs beside them.

NEBUCHADNEZZAR'S HANGING GARDENS

Students create a real-estate advertisement for Nebuchadnezzar's Hanging Gardens of Babylon.

MATERIALS

reference books, Internet access, newspaper real-estate advertisements, paper, pencils and pens

HERE'S HOW

1. Have students view Web sites about the Hanging Gardens of Babylon, such as **http://ce.eng.usf.edu/pharos/Wonders/gardens.html**.

2. Share with students the background information on page 74 about the Hanging Gardens of Babylon. Encourage students to look at reference books to gain more detailed information about the gardens.

3. Tell students to imagine that they are real-estate brokers living during the time of King Nebuchadnezzar II. Explain that the king has decided to sell the Hanging Gardens, and that students must write a real-estate advertisement for this property.

4. Have students look at real-estate ads in the newspaper as examples. Then have pairs write a real-estate ad for the Hanging Gardens. Encourage students to include an illustration in their advertisements.

EXTENSION

Have the class work together to build a model of the Hanging Gardens, using self-hardening clay and parts of plants and flowers for the gardens.

ZIGGURATS

Students use an historical account to write about a visit to a ziggurat.

MATERIALS

overhead transparency (optional), overhead projector (optional), paper, pencils or pens, colored pencils or markers, blank index cards

HERE'S HOW

1 Share with students the background information about ziggurats under "Buildings and Decorations" on page 74. Then show students the illustration of the ziggurat on this page. You may wish to make a transparency of the illustration and share it with students on an overhead projector.

2 Tell students that we know about these ziggurats because historians from long ago wrote about them. Have them compare the illustration with the following account recorded in the fifth century BC by the Greek historian Herodotus concerning a ziggurat he saw: "The courtyard of the temple complex is a square building two furlongs (1320 feet) each way, with bronze gates . . . It has a solid central tower, one furlong square, with a second erected on top of it and then a third, and so on up to eight. All eight towers can be climbed by a spiral walkway running round the outside, and about half-way up there are seats for those who make the ascent to rest on. On the summit of the topmost tower stands a great temple with a fine large couch in it, richly covered, and a golden table beside it."

3 Distribute index cards to students. Tell students to imagine that they have traveled to Mesopotamia and have seen a ziggurat. Have them use the index cards to create postcards that describe their experience to a family member or close friend. Encourage students to draw the ziggurat on one side of the postcard and to write their message on the other.

ARTS AND SCIENCES

Gilgamesh

The most famous Mesopotamian story was originally written down in about 2000 BC on clay tablets. This epic poem, called the *Epic of Gilgamesh*, told the story of Gilgamesh, King of Urak. This epic was probably based on the actual King Gilgamesh, who ruled around 3000 BC. Several tales are woven within this story, using Gilgamesh as the main focal point. This hero faces many problems involving friendship, loyalty, love of fame, adventure, death, and the quest for immortality. During Gilgamesh's adventures, he forms a friendship with the wild man Enkidu. They go off on an adventure and conquer Humbaba, the monster in the forest. Impressed, Ishtar—the goddess of love and war—asks Gilgamesh to be her husband, but he refuses. The gods strike down Enkidu with a sickness and he dies. Gilgamesh fears his own mortality and sets out to find eternal life. He journeys to find Utnapishtim, a survivor of the Great Flood, who knows the secret of immortality. From Utnapishtim, Gilgamesh learns of a plant that will keep him young. Gilgamesh obtains the plant, but it is snatched away from him by a serpent. At the end, Gilgamesh finds immortality in remembrance of his name and deeds.

The Royal Game of Ur

The Royal Game of Ur, which dates back to about 3000 BC, has been found in many parts of the ancient world, including India and Egypt. One beautiful game board that dates to about 2600 BC was found in a tomb at Ur by Sir Leonard Woolley. This game board now resides in the British Museum in London. Great care was taken to decorate these game boards, using geometric designs and precious stones. While archaeologists and scholars are not completely sure about how the Royal Game of Ur was played, they have found cuneiform tablets that explain some of the rules.

Mesopotamian Math

Mesopotamians wrote mathematics in cuneiform on clay tablets. They used a base 60 system that included place value. This system can still be seen in our 60-minute hour, 60-second minute, and the circle measuring 360 degrees. Mesopotamians used algebra and geometry, including the use of fractions, squares, and square roots. They used the Pythagorean theorem before the Greek philosopher Phythagoras even lived. All Mesopotamian numerals were written with two basic symbols: one that looked like a Y to represent one, and one that looked like a "less than" sign (<) to represent ten. Although Mesopotamians did not have a symbol for zero, they often left a space to indicate the placement of zero.

THE STORY OF GILGAMESH

Students perform a play based on the Epic of Gilgamesh.

MATERIALS

Gilgamesh: A Play (pages 81–83)

HERE'S HOW

1. Share with students the background information about Gilgamesh on page 79. Tell students that they will perform a play that is based on the latter part of the *Epic of Gilgamesh*.

2. Read to students the following summary of the first part of the epic: "King Gilgamesh of Urak is a cruel ruler. His people pray to the gods, who send the wild man Enkidu to Earth. Enkidu falls in love with Shamhat, becomes civilized, and travels to Urak. There he befriends Gilgamesh. The two travel to a cedar forest, where they kill the monster, Humbaba, who curses Enkidu. The friends cut trees and float down the Euphrates on a cedar raft to Urak. Impressed by these heroic acts, the goddess Ishtar asks Gilgamesh to be her husband, but he refuses. Upset, Ishtar urges her father to send the Bull of Heaven to wreak havoc on Uruk. Gilgamesh and Enkidu kill the bull, angering Ishtar. The gods send illness to Enkidu, who dies. A sad Gilgamesh knows that he will also die one day and searches for immortality."

3. Distribute copies of *Gilgamesh: A Play* to students and divide the class into groups to read and perform the play. (Some students may need to take two parts to cover all the roles.)

4. After students have performed the play, lead them in a discussion about how the playwright's version differs from the actual epic, which ends as follows: "In his quest for immortality, Gilgamesh searches for Utnapishtim and his wife—the only people to have survived the great flood. After traveling, Gilgamesh reaches a tavern run by Siduri, who tells Gilgamesh how to find Urshababi, a ferryman for Utnapishtim. Gilgamesh finds Urshabibi, but destroys objects needed to cross the Waters of Death. Urshabibi tells Gilgamesh to create poles for a boat, so that he will not touch the waters and die. After a dangerous journey, Gilgamesh reaches Utnapishtim, who tells him the story of the seven-day flood, how he lived by building a boat, and how the gods made him and his wife immortal. Utnapishtim tells Gilgamesh that he can be immortal if he stays awake for six days and seven nights. Gilgamesh falls asleep, but Utnapishtim's wife pleads on Gilgamesh's behalf. Utnapishtim tells Gilgamesh about a plant that will make him young. Gilgamesh finds the plant at the sea's bottom and decides to take it to Uruk to test on an old man. Urshanabi takes Gilgamesh across the Waters of Death. While they sleep, a snake eats the plant—which is why snakes shed their skins. Gilgamesh returns to his city and accepts his mortality." *(Students may note that the play differs from the epic in these ways: in the play, Siduri lends Gilgamesh the boat and there is no ferryman, Gilgamesh must stay awake while Utnapishtim tells his story, Utnapishtim's wife is missing, Ishtar is the snake, and Enkidu appears as a bird.)*

Name _____   Date _____

GILGAMESH: A PLAY

Cast in order of appearance:

Narrator

Gilgamesh: the King of Uruk

Siduri: a female tavern owner

Waters of Death: devours anyone who tries to cross it

Utnapishtim: the only human to have obtained immortality

Ishtar: the goddess of love and war

Enkidu: a friend of Gilgamesh

Scene I *(a tavern)*

(Enter Gilgamesh and Siduri)

Narrator: After the sad death of his closest friend, Enkidu, Gilgamesh sets out on a quest to find immortality. He has traveled far, but his determination will not allow him to quit. He arrives at a tavern and knocks on the door.

Gilgamesh: *(knocks on the tavern door)* Please let me in. I'm Gilgamesh, the king of Uruk.

Siduri: *(opens the door)* You don't look like any king to me. Why are your clothes ragged and why has your hair grown wild? *(She becomes suspicious and whispers to herself.)* Maybe I should bolt the door; he could be a criminal!

Gilgamesh: Please don't lock me out! I'm looking for Utnapishtim, the only human to have obtained immortality.

Siduri: I'm sorry, but he is unavailable. He lives on an island surrounded by the Waters of Death. You'll never make it across. Only the sun can cross the deadly waters.

Gilgamesh: If you will only lend me your boat, I know that I can reach him.

Siduri: Every oar that touches the deadly water will be swallowed up. You can't make it!

Gilgamesh: Then I'll cut down every tree to make a thousand oars!

Narrator: Siduri agrees to lend him her boat and Gilgamesh leaves.

Scene II *(Gilgamesh in a boat on the Waters of Death)*

Narrator: Gilgamesh sets out on the Waters of Death in Siduri's boat. He has a large supply of poles, which he cut before entering the water.

Gilgamesh: Why do you keep swallowing up every pole I dip into your dark waters?

GILGAMESH: A PLAY (Continued)

**Waters of
Death:** Don't you see that you have angered me? No one can pass through my waters except the sun.

Gilgamesh: What are these bones that fill the waters surrounding my boat? I can see them for miles!

**Waters of
Death:** Those are my trophies. They tried to pass through the waters just like you, and they found the fate that you, too, will find.

Narrator: Harsh winds begin to blow, but that makes Gilgamesh even more determined!

Gilgamesh: I just used my last oar! I must reach the island. I can see it in the distance! I can't give up now! Maybe I could make a sail with my shirt. Yes, yes, I think it's my only chance.

Narrator: Gilgamesh quickly takes off his shirt and holds it up as a sail as if to defy the winds.

Scene III *(the shores of the island, where Utnapishtim lives)*

Narrator: Meanwhile, up on top of a cliff, Utnapishtim looks out on the Waters of Death and suddenly sees the boat. He becomes very excited and begins talking to himself.

Utnapishtim: Who is that coming this way? I can't believe his boat is reaching my shore! I must hurry down off this cliff to see this magnificent creature!

Narrator: Utnaptishtim hurries down from the cliff and arrives on the beach just as the boat reaches the shore.

Utnapishtim: Are you a god or a man?

Gilgamesh: I am Gilgamesh, the King of Uruk. I have come to learn the secret of immortality.

Utnapishtim: Don't be foolish. Only gods live forever. I'm sorry, but I can't help you.

Gilgamesh: But you, yourself, were once human like me. You now have immortality. How did you do it? I want it, too!

Utnapishtim: There is only one way for you to find out: if you promise to stay awake for six days and seven nights while I read my story, which is carved on this wall. *(He points to the wall.)* If you pass this test, you will also be immortal.

Gilgamesh: I promise.

Utnapishtim: Very well. Long, long ago . . .

Narrator: Utnapishtim tells the story of his days as a king, when his people became very evil.

GILGAMESH: A PLAY (Continued)

Utnapishtim: The gods decided to send a flood to punish the people, but I was forewarned. So I built an ark to protect my family, and two of every animal. It rained for six days and seven nights and flooded the earth. When the rain stopped, my boat came to rest on a mountain, and I let out all the animals. At that very moment, the gods rewarded my wife and me with immortality.

Narrator: As Utnapishtim finishes his story; he looks over at Gilgamesh only to find that he has fallen asleep.

Utnapishtim: Gilgamesh! *(nudges him)*

Gilgamesh: Oh, I'm terribly sorry! I didn't mean to fall asleep. Please let me have another chance to gain immortality.

Utnapishtim: I'm sorry, Gilgamesh, you will never gain immortality. But there is a plant that grows in the deep waters that will keep you young as long as you live.

Scene IV *(the Waters of Death and a nearby island)*

Narrator: Gilgamesh wastes no time. Utnapishtim tells him that he will find the plant in a glowing spot in the Waters of Death. Gilgamesh dives down and struggles with the plant.

Gilgamesh: There, I have the plant! I do not have immortality, but I will at least be able to enjoy the strength of my youth after eating this plant.

Narrator: Gilgamesh gets back into his boat and then decides to rest on a nearby island. While he is sleeping, Ishtar—disguised as a snake—creeps near Gilgamesh.

Ishtar: Oh, now I can have my revenge! Gilgamesh, this is what you get for not marrying me when you had the chance! *(eats the entire plant)*

Gilgamesh: *(stretching and waking)* Where's my plant? Ishtar! How dare you take this plant! You've taken everything from me!

Narrator: All of a sudden, Enkidu appears as a bird and encourages Gilgamesh to ride on his back as he flies.

Enkidu: Gilgamesh, I want to show you your kingdom from the sky.

Gilgamesh: *(pointing down)* Hey, there are the beautiful gardens! Oh, and I see the great temples and houses! This is truly magnificent!

Enkidu: See, Gilgamesh—your kingdom is your immortality! Your city will live forever in history.

The End

THE ROYAL GAME OF UR

Students play the Royal Game of Ur, a Mesopotamian game.

MATERIALS

The Royal Game of Ur Game Board (page 85), four stones (each stone has one painted white dot), seven white circles and seven black circles (these might be round markers from another board game or cut-out paper circles)

HERE'S HOW

1 Arrange students in pairs. Give each pair one copy of *The Royal Game of Ur Game Board.* Have students speculate on ways the game might be played.

2 Share with students the background information about the game on page 79. You may wish to make a transparency of the diagram on this page and share it with students on an overhead projector.

3 Clarify the rules for students as follows:

- The game is played by two players. Each player is assigned seven white pieces or seven black pieces. The goal of the game is for players to move all of their pieces to their finish line.

- Players begin, each entering one piece, and move their pieces as shown in the diagram.

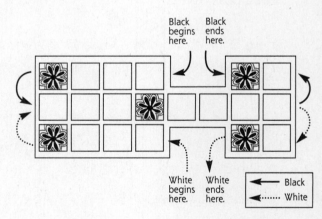

- Players roll the four stones and move their pieces the total number of dots shown. It is possible to roll at the maximum a four, and at minimum a zero.

- New pieces may enter the game as soon as the starting square is empty.

- Only one piece is allowed on each square. If a player lands on an opponent's piece, the opponent's piece is bumped off unless it is on a rosette square. All rosette squares are safe areas. When a piece is bumped off, it is taken off the board and must start back at the beginning.

- If a player cannot move a piece because the player's own pieces are blocking the move, that player loses a turn.

- Players who land on a rosette square get another turn.

- Players must throw the correct number to exit the board. The first player to move all of his or her pieces to the finish wins.

84

The Royal Game of Ur Game Board

EARLY MATHEMATICIANS

Students use Mesopotamian numerals to solve math problems.

MATERIALS

Mesopotamian Math Symbols (page 87), *Mesopotamian Math Problems* (page 88), pencils

HERE'S HOW

1. Share with students the background information about Mesopotamian Math on page 79.

2. Give students copies of *Mesopotamian Math Symbols* and *Mesopotamian Math Problems*.

3. Have students look at the chart on *Mesopotamian Math Symbols*. Explain that these symbols are numerals used by Mesopotamians. Point out that Mesopotamian numerals were written in a variety of ways, and that this chart shows only one way to write them. Ask students to point out any patterns that they see on the chart.

4. Explain to students that ▼ equaled 1 and ◁ equaled 10. Show how these symbols were combined to form numerals by pointing out examples on *Mesopotamian Math Symbols*.

5. Remind students that we use Arabic numerals and a base ten number system that includes places for hundreds, tens, ones, and other increments of ten. Tell students that the Mesopotamians used a base 60 number system. Point out that when the number 60 was reached, the symbol for 1 (▼) was used again. Explain that to avoid confusion, Mesopotamians moved the symbol ▼ one column over when it stood for 60. Point out that we use place values as well—for example, we place the numeral 6 in the tens column to indicate when it stands for 6 tens or 60.

6. Ask students how they would write the number 70 using Arabic numerals (*70*). Discuss how to write 70 using a base 60 number system. First break down 70 into powers of 60 (*60 + 10*). Then show students how to write the Mesopotamian numeral as ▼◁.

7. Tell students to solve the equations on *Mesopotamian Math Problems*, using *Mesopotamian Math Symbols* as a reference. First, direct students to identify the Mesopotamian numerals with Arabic numerals. Then ask them to solve the problems, writing the final answers for each problem using both Arabic and Mesopotamian numerals.

EXTENSION

Have students post their own math problems on the board for others to solve.

Answers

1. 3 + 5 = 8 or ▼▼▼ 2. 6 − 2 = 4 or ▼▼ 3. 11 − 1 = 10 or ◁ 4. 3 x 10 = 30 or ◁◁◁ 5. 4 x 20 = 80 or ▼◁◁

Name _____   Date _____

MESOPOTAMIAN MATH SYMBOLS

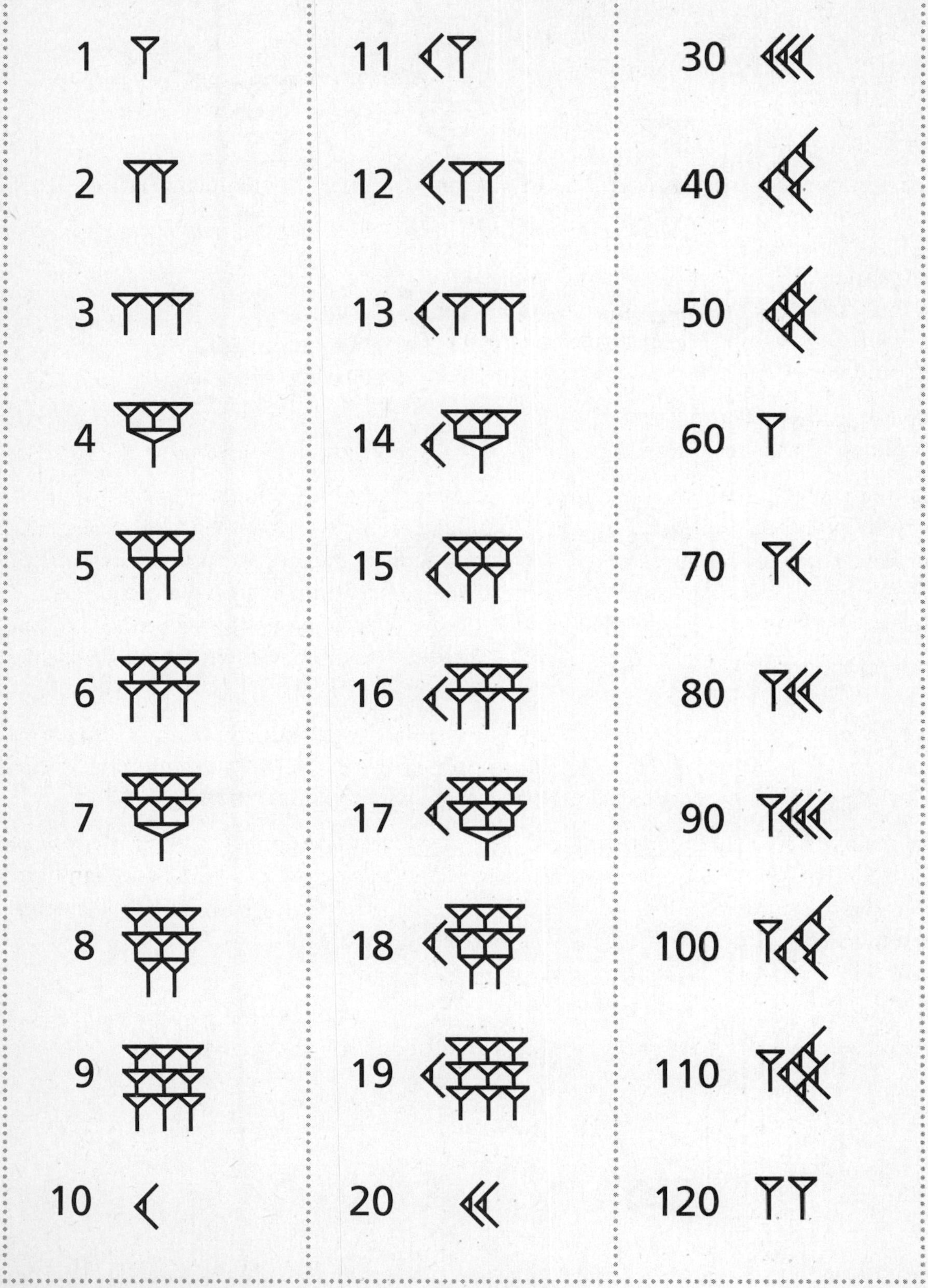

1	11	30
2	12	40
3	13	50
4	14	60
5	15	70
6	16	80
7	17	90
8	18	100
9	19	110
10	20	120

Ancient Civilizations: China, India, Africa, Mesopotamia Scholastic Teaching Resources

87

Name _____   Date _____

MESOPOTAMIAN MATH PROBLEMS

Write the corresponding Arabic numeral under each Mesopotamian symbol. Next, solve the math problems with Mesopotamian and Arabic numerals.

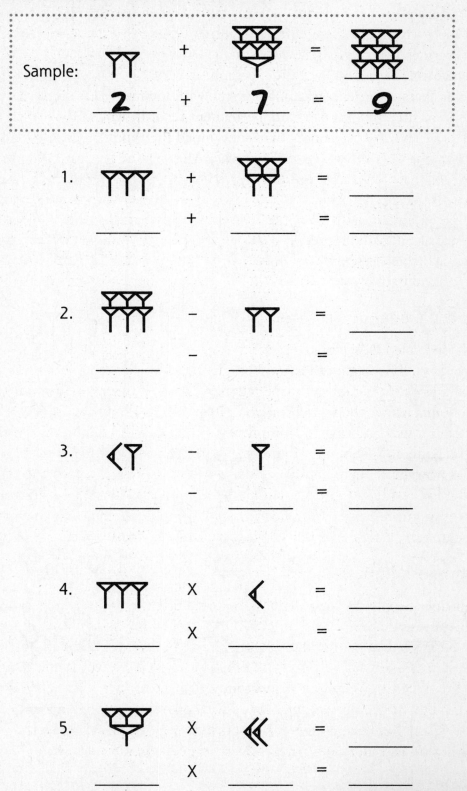

Sample: ⟨symbol⟩ + ⟨symbol⟩ = ⟨symbol⟩

2 + **7** = **9**

1.   ⟨symbol⟩ + ⟨symbol⟩ = _____

     ___ + ___ = ___

2.   ⟨symbol⟩ − ⟨symbol⟩ = _____

     ___ − ___ = ___

3.   ⟨symbol⟩ − ⟨symbol⟩ = _____

     ___ − ___ = ___

4.   ⟨symbol⟩ X ⟨symbol⟩ = _____

     ___ X ___ = ___

5.   ⟨symbol⟩ X ⟨symbol⟩ = _____

     ___ X ___ = ___

Ancient Civilizations: China, India, Africa, Mesopotamia Scholastic Teaching Resources

GOVERNMENT AND RELIGION

Cuneiform

Cuneiform was a type of writing used by ancient Mesopotamians. These symbols could be read by people who spoke many different languages, and they were pronounced differently in various languages. The earliest cuneiform clay tablets date from about 3500 BC. Cuneiform developed over time, beginning with pictographs and progressing toward abstract characters. Mesopotamians wrote with long reeds on damp clay tablets. Some tablets were fired in kilns to create permanent records, while others were used again. Scholars believe that Mesopotamians developed the simple lines of cuneiform because pictographs were difficult to draw in clay. Mesopotamians also began to use a new type of stylus with a wedge tip. About 600 cuneiform characters were used to represent sounds, ideas, and objects. While pictographs were read vertically, cuneiform symbols were read horizontally from left to right. Cuneiform was used to record a variety of information including trade, business activities, religious activities, stories, and letters. Some cuneiform tablets include important government documents, such as the Code of Hammurabi.

Hammurabi's Code

Hammurabi, who ruled Babylonia from 1792 BC to 1750 BC, created one of the first written sets of laws. The Code of Hammurabi, based on earlier laws, was written in cuneiform on a large eight-foot tall stone pillars, or *stele*. At the top of the stele, Hammurabi stands before the seated sun god, Shamash. As the guardian of justice, Shamash extends a staff and ring to Hammurabi. The Code of Hammurabi begins by addressing the gods, and mentions Hammurabi's military successes. The laws, which range in areas from business to family, include punishments for breaking the laws. Hammurabi knew that being a good king meant being fair to his people. Scholars have been able to glean much information about ancient Mesopotamians by studying the Code of Hammurabi, which emphasizes that the strong not take advantage of the weak.

Mesopotamian Religion

Like other ancient peoples, Mesopotamians believed that the forces of nature were controlled by various deities. The senior gods were called the Anunnakku and the junior gods the Igigi. The gods had different names in different Mesopotamian cultures. For example, the highest god—the sky god—was called An by the Sumerians and Anu by the Akkadians. One of the most important goddesses was the deity of motherhood, Ninhursaga. This goddess was also known by many other names, including Mami and Ninmah. Mesopotamian priests implored the help of the gods and goddesses, who had their own private lives, argued, and often fought in battles.

RECORDING TRADE WITH CUNEIFORM

Students write cuneiform on a clay tablet.

MATERIALS

The Development of Cuneiform (page 91), *Mesopotamian Math Symbols* (page 87), clay, wooden skewers or toothpicks

HERE'S HOW

1. Distribute to students *The Development of Cuneiform.* Have students view the cuneiform writing on the page. Ask students whether they can tell how some cuneiform symbols evolved by looking at the chart. Point out that the top column contains pictographs, while the middle column shows more abstract symbols of the pictographs. Help students to understand how the bottom column shows the characters further simplified and rotated 90 degrees so they could read horizontally, rather than vertically. Share with students the background information about cuneiform on page 89.

2. Distribute to students *Mesopotamian Math Symbols,* clay, and writing instruments such as wooden skewers or toothpicks.

3. Tell students that they are government workers in ancient Mesopotamia, and that their job is to record trade transactions in cuneiform. Explain to students that before the development of cuneiform numerals, people used tokens to keep track of trade. For example, three fish tokens would represent three fish. Explain that with the development of cuneiform, the symbol for three was placed next to the symbol for the trade item.

4. Using *The Development of Cuneiform* as a reference, have students select an item for their trade transaction. Direct students to use their writing instruments to write their items in cuneiform on clay.

5. Have students refer to *Mesopotamian Math Symbols* to find the correct cuneiform numeral to reflect how many of their items have been traded. Direct students to record that numeral in cuneiform next to their trade item.

6. When all students have finished, lay the tablets out on a table and number them with sticky-notes. Have students record the sticky-note numbers on a sheet of paper and next to each number, write the correct number and trade item for each tablet. Check the answers as a class.

Name _____   Date _____

THE DEVELOPMENT OF CUNEIFORM

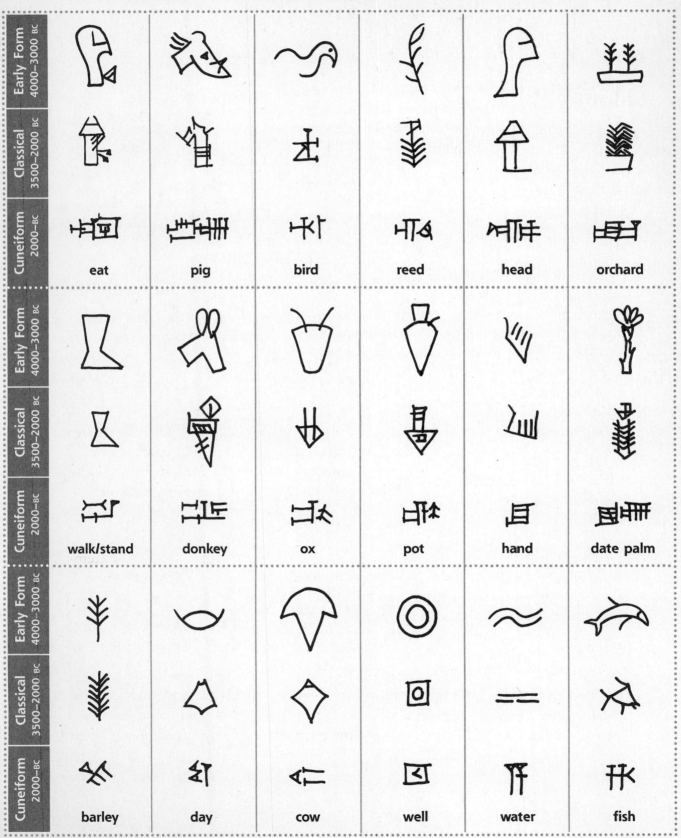

	eat	pig	bird	reed	head	orchard
Early Form 4000–3000 BC						
Classical 3500–2000 BC						
Cuneiform 2000– BC						

	walk/stand	donkey	ox	pot	hand	date palm
Early Form 4000–3000 BC						
Classical 3500–2000 BC						
Cuneiform 2000– BC						

	barley	day	cow	well	water	fish
Early Form 4000–3000 BC						
Classical 3500–2000 BC						
Cuneiform 2000– BC						

HAMMURABI'S CODE OF LAWS

Students examine Hammurabi's code and construct a code of laws for their classroom.

MATERIALS

Excerpts From Hammurabi's Code (page 93); paper; pencils or pens; large butcher paper; markers, crayons, or colored pencils

HERE'S HOW

1. Ask students to discuss the meaning of justice.

2. Share with students the background information about the Code of Hammurabi on page 89. Distribute *Excerpts From Hammurabi's Code* for students to read. Allow students to share their ideas about these laws.

3. Explain that archaeologists and historians have used the Code of Hammurabi to explain how ancient Mesopotamians lived. Tell students that they will act as scholars to glean information about ancient Mesopotamians using the Code of Hammurabi.

4. Have students write on a piece of paper their ideas about ancient Mesopotamians. Ask them to consider what life under the rule of these laws might be like.

5. Allow students to share their ideas with the class.

6. Ask students to think about rules that could make their classroom a better place. Let students work in small groups to brainstorm a code of laws for their classroom. Have groups write their ideas on large butcher paper using colored pencils, crayons, or markers. Then have them present their codes to the class. Ask the class to vote on the most just code to govern the classroom.

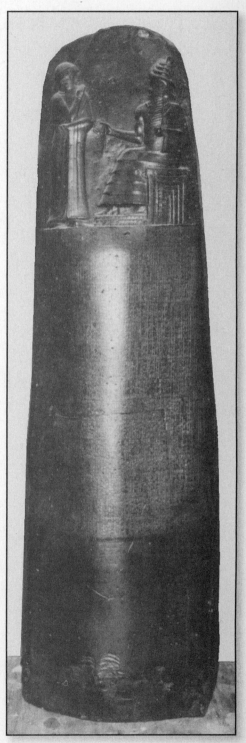

© Wendy Conklin

EXCERPTS FROM HAMMURABI'S CODE

The Code of Hammurabi included 282 laws. Here are some of them.

1.   If a man accuses another of murder but does not prove it, the accuser shall be killed.

2.   If a citizen has charged another citizen with sorcery but has not proven it, the one charged with sorcery shall go to the river and throw himself in. If the river overwhelms him, his accuser shall take possession of his estate. If the river clears that citizen of guilt and he remains safe, the one who accused him of sorcery shall be put to death and the one who threw himself into the river shall take possession of his accuser's estate.

8.   If a man has stolen an ox, a sheep, a donkey, a pig, or a boat belonging to a god (or) to the palace, he shall pay thirty times its value; if it belonged to a common man, he shall pay ten times its value. If the thief does not have enough to pay, he shall be killed.

56.   If a man opens a water supply and the water sweeps away the work on the neighboring field, he shall measure out ten kur of grain for each burum (of land).

109.   If there is a woman tavern keeper who allows criminals to gather in her tavern and she does not arrest them and take them to the palace, that tavern keeper shall be killed.

127.   If a man accuses a priestess or the wife of another man of wrongdoing, but does not prove it, that man shall be beaten in the presence of the judges and half of his hair shall be shaved off.

186.   If a man adopts a young boy who (later) searches for his father and mother, that child may return to his father's house.

195.   If a son strikes his father, the son's hand shall be cut off.

218.   If a physician performs a major operation with a bronze instrument on a man and causes the man's death, or if he opens the citizen's temple with a bronze instrument and destroys the man's eye, the physician's hand shall be cut off.

227.   If a man deceives a barber and the barber shaves off the slave-mark of a slave who does not belong to him, that man shall be killed and hung at his doorway; the barber shall swear, "I did not shave it off knowingly" and shall then be released.

A Mural of Mesopotamian Gods

Students create a mural that illustrates a Mesopotamian creation myth.

Materials

mural paper, tape, pencils, paper, colored markers

Here's How

1. Tape or tack mural paper on the wall. Share with students the background information about ancient Mesopotamian religions on page 89.

2. Write the following Mesopotamian deities on the board:
The Anunnakku
    Anu: sky
    Enlil: Earth
    Enki: ocean
The Igigi

3. Tell students the following Mesopotamian myth about the creation of people:

Before people walked the earth, Anu ruled the sky, Enlil ruled the earth, and Enki ruled the ocean. These were the senior gods, or Anunnakku, who forced the lesser gods, or Igigi, to work for them. The Anunnakku forced the Igigi to dig the Tigris and Euphrates rivers, as well as many canals. After 3,600 years, the Igigi rebelled outside the home of Enlil. Alarmed, Enlil held a conference with the other Anunnakku. They decided to create a creature to do some of the Igigi's work. Enki directed the mother goddess, Mami, to make a creature by mixing the blood of a junior god with clay. Together Mami and Enki created seven men and seven women. However, because they made people from a lesser god, the people were flawed and often caused trouble on Earth.

4. Tell students that they will create a mural of this myth. Divide students into six groups to work on different parts of the mural. Assign the sections as follows: (a) the Anunnakku, consisting of Anu, Enlil, and Enki; (b) the Igigi digging the Tigris and Euphrates rivers and canals; (c) the Igigi rebelling in front of Enlil's home; (d) a conference of the Anunnakku; (e) Enki and Mami creating the first people; (f) people causing trouble on Earth.

5. Direct students to sketch out their sections of the mural on a piece of paper before drawing it on the mural paper. When students have completed their sketches, have them transfer them to the mural paper. Have students color their sections of the mural with markers.

6. Invite another class to view the mural. Have each group present their section of the mural, recounting the entire myth to your visitors.

BIBLIOGRAPHY

CHINA

Books

Cotterell, Arthur. *Ancient China (Eyewitness Books)*. DK Publishing, 2005.

Goldstein, Peggy. *Long Is a Dragon*. Pacific View Press, 1992.

Lee, Jeanne M., translator. *The Song of Mu Lan*. Front Street, 1991.

Lindesay, William. *The Terracotta Army of the First Emperor of China*. Odyssey, 1999.

O'Connor, Jane. *The Emperor's Silent Army: Terracotta Warriors of Ancient China*. Viking, 2002.

Web Sites

Ancient China: The British Museum **http://www.ancientchina.co.uk/menu.html**

China: Minnesota State University **http://www.mnsu.edu/emuseum/prehistory/china**

Chinese Robes: Kent State University Museum **http://dept.kent.edu/museum/project/Erin/symbol1.htm**

Daily Life in Ancient China **http://members.aol.com/Donnclass/Chinalife.html**

Terra Cotta Warriors **http://campus.northpark.edu/history/WebChron/China/TerraWar.html**

INDIA

Books

Kirkpatrick, Naida. *The Indus Valley* (Understanding People in the Past). Heinemann Library, 2002.

Sharma, Bulbul. *The Ramayana for Children*. Penguin, 2004.

Schomp, Virginia. *Ancient India* (People of the Ancient World). Franklin Watts, 2005.

Stewart, Melissa. *Science in Ancient India* (Science in History). Franklin Watts, 1999.

Weitzman, David. *Rama and Sita: A Tale from Ancient Java*. David R. Godine, 2002.

Web Sites

Ancient India: Minnesota State University **http://www.mnsu.edu/emuseum/prehistory/india/index.shtml**

Ancient India: The British Museum **http://www.ancientindia.co.uk/menu.html**

Ancient India: Washington State University **http://www.wsu.edu/~dee/ANCINDIA/CONTENTS.HTM**

The Ancient Indus Valley **http//www.harappa.com/har/har0.html**

Indus Valley Civilization **http://www.sscnet.ucla.edu/southasia/History/Ancient/Indus.html**

BIBLIOGRAPHY (Continued)

AFRICA

Books

Brooks, Lester. *Great Civilizations of Ancient Africa*. Four Winds Press, 1971.

Jenkins, Earnestine. *A Glorious Past: Ancient Egypt, Ethiopia, and Nubia* (Milestones in Black History). Chelsea House, 1995.

Joseph, Joan. *Black African Empires* (First Books). Scholastic Library, 1974.

Kassinger, Ruth. *Iron and Steel*. 21st Century Books, 2003.

Mann, Kenny. *Egypt, Kush, Aksum: Northeast Africa* (African Kingdoms of the Past). Silver Burdett, 1996.

Service, Pamela F. *The Ancient African Kingdom of Kush* (Cultures of the Past). Benchmark Books, 1998.

Web Sites

Ancient Africa's Black Kingdoms **http://www.homestead.com/wysinger/ancientafrica.html**

Ancient Nubia: Egypt's Rival in Africa
http://www.umich.edu/~kelseydb/Exhibits/AncientNubia/Artifacts.html

Black Kingdoms of the Nile **http://www.pbs.org/wonders/Episodes/Epi1/1_wondr2.htm**

Dig Nubia: Exploring the Science of Archaeology **http://www.dignubia.org**

Nubia Salvage Project **http://www.oi.uchicago.edu/OI/PROJ/NUB/Nubia.html**

MESOPOTAMIA

Books

Ali, Daud, et al. *Great Civilizations of the East: Ancient Japan, Ancient India, the Chinese Empire, Mesopotamia*. Anness, 2003.

Moss, Carol. *Science in Ancient Mesopotamia*. Scholastic Library, 1999.

Zeman, Ludmila. *Gilgamesh the King* (Gilgamesh Trilogy). Tundra, 1998.

———. *The Revenge of Ishtar* (Gilgamesh Trilogy). Tundra, 1998.

———. *The Last Quest of Gilgamesh* (Gilgamesh Trilogy). Tundra, 1998.

Web Sites

Architectural Marvels of Ancient Mesopotamia
http://www.faculty.fairfield.edu/jmac/meso/meso.htm

Mesopotamia: The British Museum **http://www.mesopotamia.co.uk/menu.html**

The Oriental Institute of the University of Chicago Museum Education Teacher Resource Center (TRC) **http://www-oi.uchicago.edu/OI/MUS/ED/TRC/trc_home.html**

The Development of Writing **http://www.mesopotamia.co.uk/writing/story/page01.html**